KU-260-492

INSIGHT POCKET GUIDE

SeYCHeLLeS

Discovery
CHANNEL

APA PUBLICATIONS L
Part of the Langenscheidt Publishing Group

Seychelles and the Inner Islands

16 km / 10 miles

 Bird Island

 Denis

I n d i a n

O c e a n

Aride

Curieuse

Petite Soeur Grand Soeur

Cousin Anse Volbert

Félicité

Cousine Grand Anse Baie Ste Anne La Reunion Marianne

Praslin

La Digue

North

Anse la Passe

Mamelles

Grand Barbe *Silhouette*

Brisare Rocks

Île Aux Récifs *Frégate*

Beau Vallon Bay Beau Vallon St Anne L'Îlot Frégate

Round Moyenne

Victoria Long

Cerf

Conception Cascade ✈ *Mahé*

Thérèse Grand Anse

Anse Aux Pins

Anse Royal

Anse À La Mouche Anse Royale

Baie Lazare

Takamaka

*S e y c h e l l e s
B a n k*

Welcome!

This guidebook combines the interests and enthusiasms of two of the world's best-known information providers: Insight Guides, who have set the standard for visual travel guides since 1970, and Discovery Channel, the world's premier source of non-fiction television programming. Its aim is to bring you the best of Seychelles in a series of itineraries devised by two of Insight's Seychelles correspondents Judith and Adrian Skerrett.

The tailor-made itineraries in this book will help you get the most out of Seychelles. Mahé and Praslin are the obvious hubs for your exploration: full-day drives through these islands reveal their secrets. Or else, opt for a morning tour of the capital, an afternoon exploring a coco de mer forest, or a whole day chasing a sailfish, snorkelling or discovering an uninhabited island. There are giant tortoises and rare birds to find, ox carts to ride and fresh fish to barbecue. The itineraries to the remote coral islands of Bird, Desroches and Alphonse are perfect for getting away from it all. If you've come to cruise, sail, dive, fish or hike, a separate Activities section covers these possibilities. Chapters on history and culture, eating out and nightlife, and a useful practical information section complete this reader-friendly guide.

Judith and Adrian Skerrett first washed up on the pristine shores of Seychelles in 1980, intending to live and work for just two years. Many years later, however, charmed by the magical attractions of the islands, they are still there. Both keen naturalists and authors of several guides on the Seychelles, the Skerretts love the stunning natural beauty of their adopted home, describing some of the idyllic islands as 'the stuff of dreams'.

*Pages 2/3:
dream scene,
Anse Lazio
beach on
Praslin*

C O N T E N T S

History & Culture

From the Portuguese galleons of Vasco da Gama to
pirate ships from Madagascar, from African slaves to
colonial governors – an account of the people and
forces that have shaped Seychelles **10–17**

Seychelles' Highlights

**The first 11 itineraries highlight the main
attractions of Mahé and Praslin (the largest of the
islands) and their surrounding isles. The remaining
three itineraries are excursions to the remote coral
islands of Bird, Desroches and Alphonse.**

MAHÉ

1 From Bel Ombre to Beau Vallon gives an
overview of Mahé with a full-day drive. It begins with
a detour to Bel Ombre's treasure dig, then visits Bel
Air Cemetery, a national monument containing graves
from the earliest settlement. Afterwards, it journeys
along the west coast and crosses the mountain pass
of Sans Souci to Morne Seychellois National Park...............**21**

2 Victoria and Botanical Gardens spends a
morning walking in Victoria's lush Botanical Gardens,
browsing in Sir Selwyn Selwyn Clarke Market, visiting
the museum and taking in some interesting shops **30**

**3 St Anne and Baie Ternay Marine National
Parks** spends a full day (or half day) snorkelling, and
exploring the coral reef in a glass-bottom boat or a
subsea viewer. Afterwards, a walk on Round Island or a
lazy afternoon on an idyllic beach **33**

4 Scenic Flight takes a helicopter ride over St
Anne Marine National Park and over the mountainous
Morne Seychellois National Park **34**

5 Silhouette Island focuses on a beautiful
volcanic isle, including a look at plantation life, a walk
in the hills and a cruise around dramatic cliffs **36**

6 Anonyme Island is a flexible half day tour in
which you set the timetable and activities to suit the mood ...**38**

PRASLIN

7 Valleé de Mai to Anse Lazio is a jeep tour of
Praslin, beginning at the Vallée de Mai National Park
and then taking a coastal drive to Baie Ste Anne for
lunch and local art...**41**

8 La Digue takes the ferry to visit this spectacular
granite island. Explore by bike, ox cart or on foot and
maybe see the black paradise flycatcher **45**

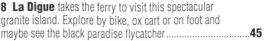

9 Aride spends the day taking a guided tour of a conservationist's paradise which teems with rare birds and exotic plants **49**

10 Cousin takes a half-day boat trip to the Cousin Island Special Reserve, a seabird island second only to Aride. Includes the possibility of continuing to Curieuse for a Creole barbecue **52**

11 Curieuse and St Pierre is a boat ride to these two islands, where you can spend your time exploring a mangrove swamp, visiting a giant land tortoise research centre and snorkelling around the coral reefs off St Pierre **53**

CORAL ISLANDS

12 Bird Island is an excursion to a remote coral island which is home to a colony of sooty terns. Attractions include fishing, beautiful beaches and good snorkelling **55**

13 Desroches is an escape to a remote coral island – the ultimate getaway paradise for divers and watersports fans **57**

14 Alphonse is a journey back in time to an old plantation on a beautiful coral atoll. Exciting diving and fly fishing, and lonely deserted beaches abound **59**

Pages 8/9: the fairy tern is an emblem of Seychelles' national airline

Activities

Five suggestions on active pursuits, from nature rambles to diving and deep-sea fishing.........................**61–67**

Shopping, Eating Out & Nightlife

Tips on what to buy, where to dine out on local specialities, and where to stay up late.............................**68–77**

Calendar of Special Events

All the events worth watching out for during a year in the Seychelles **78–79**

Practical Information

All the background information you are likely to need for your stay in the Seychelles, including a list of recommended hotels **80–93**

Maps

Seychelles and the	**Mahé**...........................22	
Inner Islands...........................4	**Victoria**............................31	
Seychelles and the	**Praslin** 40	
Indian Ocean.................18–19	**La Digue**............................45	

Index and Credits 94–96

HISTORY & CULTURE

What makes the Seychelles islands the way they are is their splendid isolation. Literally a thousand miles from anywhere – India to the north, Africa to the west, Sri Lanka to the east and Madagascar to the south – they were uninhabited until the late 18th century. Thus, while the natural beauty of other Indian Ocean islands was gradually decimated, that of the Seychelles has been preserved.

Early Contact

The first people to have contact with the Seychelles may have been Arab traders in the 9th century. There is no evidence for this as yet, but it seems unlikely that these great voyagers did not stumble upon Seychelles. When Portuguese explorer Vasco da Gama sailed across this ocean, he had an Arab pilot on board with him. The Portuguese may have learnt of Seychelles from such Arab geographers, though there is no record of the latter visiting the granitic islands.

In 1501, another famous Portuguese explorer, Jean de Nova gave his name to an island in the coralline group (now Farquhar), and in 1505, da Gama sailed through and named the Amirantes islands, but no attempt was made to colonise them.

The British, who were next on the scene, showed a similar disinterest. A merchant vessel, the *Ascension*, arrived off Mahé in January 1609. The islands appeared uninhabited to the crew on board. They reported an excellent harbour and that good supplies were available, but no one back home took the bait.

Piracy

From 1690 to 1720, many pirates were based in Madagascar. The new flow of merchant shipping in the Indian Ocean made these vessels easy prey for them. Seychelles' isolation made it an ideal hideout and it seems likely that the pirates took advantage of this to make repairs and store supplies.

Although there is no direct proof that pirates visited Seychelles, rumours of buried treasure abound on the islands. The most famous legend is that of Le Vasseur – recounted in the *Itinerary 1* –

DOM VASCO DA GAMA
1469-1524

Portuguese explorer, Vasco da Gama

10

but since the earliest settlement of the islands, there have been other tales. Many Seychellois are convinced that certain local families founded their fortunes on caches they had unearthed. On Frégate, you may come across ruins associated with pirates: in 1911, some silver coins, forks, spoons, shoebuckles and a bosun's whistle were found on Astove, an island in the Aldabra group.

However, the pirates' heyday in the region soon ended. Trading concerns with India were too important, and the English and French colonial powers sent their navies to police the area. At one time, as many as 17 pirate ships, with over 1,500 men had been active; but by 1719, a visitor to Madagascar could only find 17 men who said they were pirates – all of whom longed to go home. For every pirate who made it back to a prosperous retirement, there were dozens more who were either killed in action, murdered by rivals, drank themselves to an early grave, or starved to death when money ran out. Life under the Jolly Roger was not all 'yo ho ho and a bottle of rum!'

A wall on Frégate reputedly built by pirates

A French Possession

Trading interests in the region had already motivated the French to occupy Bourbon (Reunion) in 1663, and the Île de France (Mauritius) in 1721. They found it worrying to have the Seychelles islands, which the British might occupy, in close proximity to their bases. At the time, the French had the Indian Ocean islands to themselves and they wanted no competition on their doorstep.

In 1742, Frenchman Captain Lazare Picault was sent to report on the Seychelles. It was decided that they were of sufficient interest to merit a second voyage in 1744. This time, Picault brought back detailed charts, and named Mahé in honour of the governor of Mauritius. The name Seychelles was that of a French finance minister – Viscount Jean Moreau de Séchelles – given in 1756 when Captain Nicholas Morphey was sent to claim the islands for France.

As the governors of Mauritius were responsible for Seychelles, they had to ensure that the new colony did not cost too much. Therefore, the governors must have been pleased when Brayer du Barré, a private entrepreneur from France, undertook the settlement of Seychelles as a speculative venture. Du Barré was given little finance or

The Stone of Possession laid by the French

support. He sent 26 colonists to Seychelles in August 1770, who landed on St Anne Island. Meanwhile, somewhat sneakily, the French government decided to establish their own settlement on Mahé where Pierre Poivre, the administrator of Mauritius, encouraged the growing of spices. Slaves were brought to the island to do the hard work.

After initial success, du Barré's settlement failed. It did not have enough support from the authorities, and du Barré bankrupted himself. His settlers started making money by selling tortoises and timber to passing ships rather than farming. Many moved to Mahé and set up camps in the hills above Victoria. The government settlement at Anse Royale struggled along. In the end, most of du Barré's people were evacuated, though one man, Gillot, soldiered on alone at Anse Royale until the colony was re-established in 1778.

The Days of de Quincy

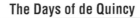

Jean Baptiste Queau de Quincy guided the colony through the difficult war years and lifted Seychelles out of the doldrums. The administrator arrived in 1793; soon after which England and France were at war. Quincy knew it would be pointless to resist: he capitulated, but only until the British warship sailed out of sight. In all, he made seven such capitulations to the English captains, a move which did not require Seychelles to become part of Britain, and guaranteed security for the property of the Seychellois. Once the ships had left, Seychelles was neutral and French warships were made welcome.

Bust of Pierre Poivre

Despite Quincy's cosy system, there were several dramatic sea battles between the English and French just off Mahé. In September 1801, the English ship *Victor* was attacked by the French corvette *La Flêche*, but she was able to bring her broadside to bear on the French ship and fire on her incessantly. *La Flêche* began to sink, but rather than see her seized by the British, the captain ran her aground on a reef and set her on fire. When the two opposing captains met ashore later, the English captain complimented his opponent on his spirited defence.

In 1801, the arrival of 70 'terrorists' deported by Napoleon from France, following an attempt on his life, caused more problems for Quincy. Many had reputations for having carried out some of the worst outrages of the Revolution. However, very few stayed here. Some escaped but the majority were re-deported to the Comores. There, most died, from uncertain causes. It may have been due to illnesses or possibly on the orders of the sultan who was not keen on potential trouble makers and gave orders to have them poisoned.

Mauritius finally fell to the British and in 1812, Seychelles became a British colony. Quincy was kept on by the British to run Seychelles. He later became a Justice of the Peace and was a respected figure in the colony until his death in 1827.

There were early, but not very serious attempts to stamp out slave trading in Seychelles. An act of 1807 had made slave trading illegal in Britain and her colonies, although it was still possible to own slaves. Full emancipation finally came in 1839 and owners were paid compensation for the slaves they had lost.

Former slaves found it was easy to live in Seychelles without working, and understandably chose not to. The ex-owners found it hard to adjust to having to pay for workers. They felt farming was almost impossible without slaves and some chose to live off their compensation payments instead. Many emigrated; others decided to plant their estates with coconut palms, since it took less labour to produce coconuts than to grow the traditional cash crops of cotton, sugar and maize. Seychelles now had the typical social structure of an ex-French colony; rich planters, or the *gran blan*, usually of French origin, who enjoyed most of the wealth while those of African descent scraped a living from the sea or small gardens where they grew vegetables. Those of mixed parentage, or the *blan koko* (the not so well-off whites), fell between the two levels.

Salvation for the economy came in the form of almost 3,000 'liberated Africans', rescued from Arab slave traders by British anti-slaving patrols on the east African coast between 1861 and 1874. They were a source of cheap labour for the plantations. Exports of coconut oil increased; vanilla also became a valuable cash crop. Seychelles prospered and the population grew steadily. In 1903, Seychelles ceased to be a dependency of Mauritius.

A National Archives list of African slaves

Then, an artificial substitute was found for vanilla, and the market price plummeted. In addition, the outbreak of World War I meant that ships could not call to collect cargoes of coconut oil. By 1918, poverty was widespread. Crime figures soared as desperate people turned to theft. New cash crops such as cinnamon oil, guano and copra were introduced and helped the colony to survive the grim war years.

Government House, Seychelles. UNE BONNE ANNÉE W. E. DAVIDSON
December 1905.

GOVERNMENT HOUSE
SEYCHELLES.

A 1905 photograph of the Government House

The Age of Politics

World War II caused more distress in the colony, leading to the formation of Seychelles' first political grouping, the Association of Seychelles Taxpayers. Although its members were mostly well-to-do planters, they spoke up against the colonial power on behalf of the Seychellois. In 1964, there was a more general politicisation of the country when the Seychelles Democratic Party (SDP) and Seychelles Peoples United Party (SPUP) were created, led by James Mancham and France Albert Rene respectively. The SDP wished to retain Seychelles' close ties with Britain, whilst the SPUP, a socialist party, pushed for full independence.

In 1967, universal adult suffrage was introduced for elections to the Legislative Council. In 1970, this council became a 15-member Legislative Assembly in which, after elections, the SDP had six seats and the SPUP five. James Mancham of the SDP was therefore made Chief Minister by the British Governor. In the 1974 elections, SDP won 52.4 percent of the votes and SPUP 46.7 percent. In 1975, there were talks in London to produce a new constitution. Seychelles was to become an autonomous colony with a coalition government: a year later, a new constitution was finalised.

Independence to the Present

In June 1976, Seychelles became an independent republic in the Commonwealth. The flamboyant Mancham became President, with Rene as Prime Minister. On 5 June 1977, with Mancham in London, the SPUP led an armed coup. A new government was formed, with Rene as President. Seychelles became a one party socialist state and the SPUP became the sole political party under the title of the Seychelles Peoples Progressive Front (SPPF).

Following the June 1977 coup, Mancham claimed he had no ambitions to return if this meant additional fighting. Other opponents of Rene were not so reticent. In May 1978, 21 Seychellois were arrested for plotting a counter-coup. Among them was Gerard

Hoareau, who was imprisoned for nine months. On release, he left the country and became the chief architect of the *Mouvement Pour La Resistance*, which surreptitiously distributed anti-government leaflets and plotted Rene's overthrow.

Rene survived several coup attempts, including a much-publicised one by mercenaries in November 1981. Rumours of an imminent counter-coup persisted, and Hoareau remained determined to topple Rene. Three years later, Hoareau was shot dead as he stepped out from his London home. The crime was never solved, but he became a martyr to the cause of the opposition.

In December 1991, Rene announced a return to multi-party politics. Mancham returned to a rousing welcome, but it was Rene who won the majority of the seats at a referendum held in July 1992 to elect a committee to draw up a new constitution. The first draft produced by SPPF was rejected in November 1992, but a second more inclusive draft was adopted in June 1993, followed the next month by Seychelles' first multi-party presidential election since June 1976. Rene defeated Mancham with 59 percent of the votes cast.

Meanwhile, with Mancham failing to regain his former influence, a new force emerged, fighting the 1998 elections as the United Opposition (UO). Rene again emerged victorious but the UO (subsequently renamed Seychelles National Party or SNP) forced Mancham into third place.

Rene called another snap presidential election in August 2001. Mancham declined to stand. Rene won again with 54 percent of votes cast, but Wavel Ramkalawan, leader of the SNP, doubled his share of the vote. In February 2004, Rene announced that after 27 years as President, he was stepping down and James Michel (elected as Vice-President in 2001) would take over as President.

Melting Pot

The Seychellois, as a people, have a short history. They were brought here from diverse backgrounds. Some came from France in search of their fortunes; others were Creoles, born in the colonies. For years, the majority of the population were voiceless slaves from Africa

Most Seychellois are Catholics

and Madagascar. By the time they were free, the islands were a British colony. This imposed a foreign veneer on the place, and national and indigeneous characteristics were suppressed.

The Seychellois culture involves a merging of European, African and Malagasy elements. This process is reflected in the Creole language, which, though based largely on French, has African, Malagasy and Arab words, and an increasing number of English ones. It originated as a *lingua franca* by which slaves from Africa and Madagascar could communicate with each other and with their French masters.

Most Seychellois are Catholics and place great emphasis on their faith. Strangely though, this has not stamped out the tradition of loose family ties, with frequent partner changes or cohabiting couples choosing not to get married until fairly late in life.

Again, despite their strong Catholic traditions, there are still traces of ancient magic left, much of which probably came from African and Madagascan tradition. Known as *grigri*, and practised by sorcerers called *bonnonm* or *bonnfanm dibwa*, this is still not a subject discussed openly. Ceremonies involve many unusual charms, such as playing cards, old tobacco tins, pebbles, mirrors and old coins, as well as chicken bones, herbal extracts and potions. A good sorcerer can cast a spell on someone to influence his judgment, create a love potion, or deal with a troublesome *dondosya* (zombie) or *nanm* (ghost). Such beliefs flourished when the islands were cut off from the world and people had nothing else to do at night but sit in the candlelight and tell stories in hushed voices. Since the advent of the cinema, radio and TV, their power has waned.

Moutya drummer

Dance and Music

Old instruments such as the *bonm* and *zez* are rarely seen, but *moutyas* are occasionally held by the light of bonfires; and no one who has seen the sensual dance can doubt its African origins. At one time, shocked government officials and church leaders tried to stamp out the *moutya*, which is a dance and social event all rolled into one. The dance is slow and sensual, although the dancers barely touch each other. The lively *sega*, now the most popular dance of the islands, is a fairly recent arrival. Its origins are African but the Indian Ocean islands have made it very much part of the Creole culture.

The European element is seen in the *kanmtole*; the robust country dances such as the *vals*, *ecossaise*, polka and *pas de quatre*, which are based on French and English courtly dances.

The Seychellois Today

Seychelles was a French colony for 45 years. It was British for over 160 years, yet the British influence seems superficial to the casual observer. The Creole language helps give the place its French feel, but the British elements are strongly reflected in the business side of the islands: the law, the institutions and commerce.

Seychellois are at home in both French and British cultures, but they have also looked beyond them. Creole cuisine is enriched by Indian and Chinese elements, brought in by settlers in the 1800s.

Historical Highlights

AD851 Possible first indication of Seychelles on Arab charts.

1501 Jean de Nova discovers and names Farquhar (formerly Jean de Nova).

1502 Vasco da Gama passes through the Amirantes. Seychelles is marked on Portuguese charts.

1609 The *Ascension*, a British ship, arrives at Mahé and finds the islands uninhabited.

1690–1720 Pirates based on Madagascar suspected to have frequented Seychelles.

1742 Lazare Picault sent to report on Seychelles for the French.

1744 Picault sent to collect more details. Mahé is named.

1756 Nicholas Morphey sent to claim the islands for France officially. The islands are named Seychelles, after a French minister.

1770 Brayer du Barré sends the first settlers. Most were later evacuated, nearly starving.

1771 The Royal Spice Garden is established on Mahé.

1778 Lieutenant de Romainville and a 15-man garrison take control of the colony. First buildings erected at *L'Etablissement* (Victoria).

1790 Creation of a Colonial Assembly to discuss local administration and the new ideas of the French Revolution.

1794 First Seychelles Capitulation signed by Commandant Quincy.

1801 Arrival of 70 political deportees from France.

1812 Seychelles becomes a British colony.

1835 Abolition of slavery in Seychelles. In an attempt to phase ex-slaves gradually into the community, they were apprenticed to their former owners until emancipation.

1839 Full emancipation of slaves.

1841 *L'Etablissement* is renamed Victoria.

1861 Arrival of the first 'liberated Africans'.

1862 The *Avalanche*, a huge landslide falls on Victoria and claims many victims. Production of coconut oil increases.

1899 Record year for exports of vanilla.

1900 King Prempeh of Ashanti exiled to Seychelles by the British; one of a series of political prisoners sent here.

1903 Seychelles becomes a Crown Colony independent of Mauritius.

1926 Electricity and telephone is introduced.

1939 Creation of Seychelles Taxpayers Association, the first opposition to the colonial administration.

1964 Creation of two political parties, the SPUP and SDP.

1967 Introduction of universal adult suffrage.

1970 The first Constitutional Congress. Creation of a Legislative Assembly. At the first election, SDP wins six seats; SPUP wins five.

1971 Opening of the international airport. Tourism becomes by far the most important source of income for Seychelles.

1976 Seychelles becomes an independent republic in the Commonwealth. Creation of a coalition government; James Mancham (SDP) is President and Albert Rene (SPUP) is Prime Minister.

1977 Coup by the SPUP overthrows Mancham's coalition government.

1978 Seychelles becomes a single party state led by the Seychelles People's Progressive Front (SPPF).

1981 An attempt to overthrow Rene by mercenaries led by 'Mad Mike' Hoareau fails.

1982 A mutiny in the army is quelled with the help of Tanzanian troops.

1991 A return to a multi-party system is announced.

1992 First draft constitution fails to secure 60 percent of the votes at the referendum.

1993 Second draft constitution adopted. Rene wins first multi-party presidential election.

1998 Rene re-elected President. SPPF retains majority in Congress, United Opposition taking three seats and DP one.

2001 Rene re-elected President but with a much reduced margin of victory.

2004 Rene announces he will step down, passing the Presidency to his Vice-President James Michel.

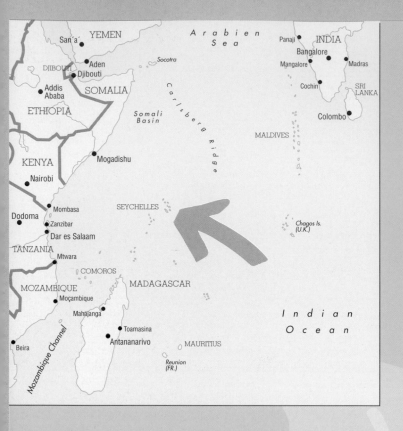

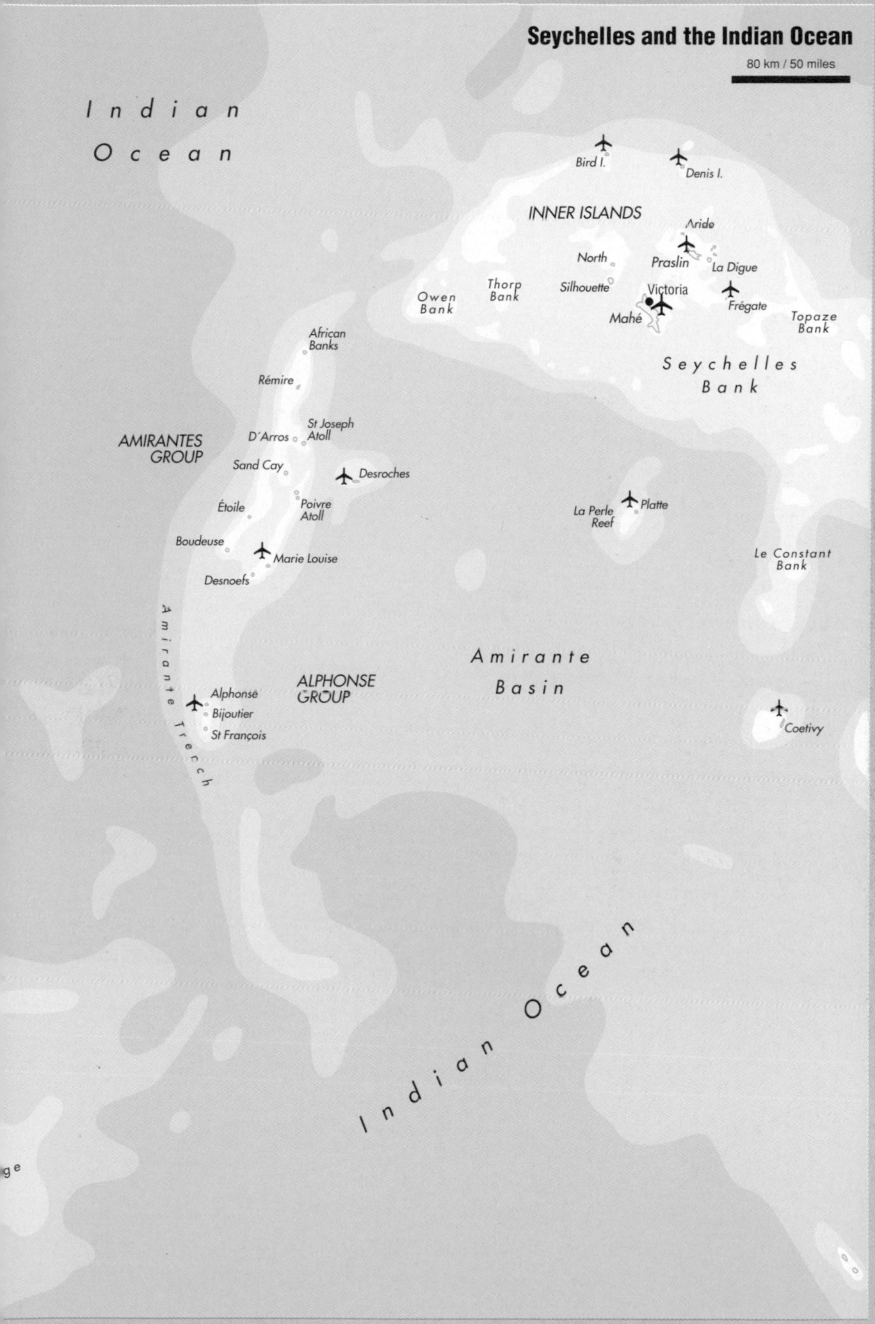

Seychelles and the Indian Ocean

80 km / 50 miles

Indian
Ocean

Bird I. ✈   ✈ Denis I.

INNER ISLANDS

Aride

North   Praslin   La Digue

Owen   Thorp   Silhouette   Victoria ✈
Bank   Bank   Mahé   ✈ Frégate
                                        Topaze
                                        Bank

Seychelles
Bank

African
Banks

Rémire

AMIRANTES   D´Arros   St Joseph
GROUP   Atoll

Sand Cay   ✈ Desroches

Étoile   Poivre
          Atoll   La Perle   ✈ Platte
Boudeuse   Reef
          ✈ Marie Louise   Le Constant
Desnoefs   Bank

Amirante
Basin

Alphonse   ALPHONSE
✈ Bijoutier   GROUP   ✈
St François   Coetivy

Indian Ocean

ge

Mahé

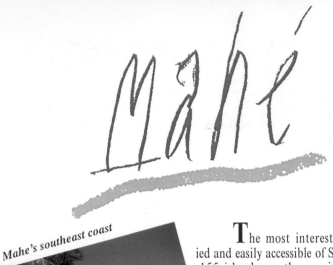

Mahe's southeast coast

The most interesting, varied and easily accessible of Seychelles' 155 islands are the granitic group of 39 islands. Known as the Inner Islands of Seychelles, the main islands in this group are Mahé, Praslin and La Digue. As the Inner Islands lie within a relatively small area, they can be explored using Mahé and Praslin – the two largest islands – as bases.

Wherever you fly from, you will arrive at Mahé, the largest and highest island of Seychelles with an area of 155sq km (60sq miles). This is the most developed island, the commercial centre and home to 90 percent of Seychellois. Yet, the mountains are verdant with dense forest, the beaches are superb, and it has the best facilities to enjoy watersports and game fishing.

Many visitors rush away to Praslin, La Digue or even further afield, in the belief they must escape Mahé quickly to discover the real Seychelles. This is a mistake. Mahé is beautiful in its own right and the best base from which to plan excursions to most other islands, including the coral islands Silhouette, St Anne Marine National Park and other interesting areas.

The stunning Beau Vallon beach is where many tourists stay, yet it is far from crowded. Mass tourism has not arrived in Seychelles. North of Beau Vallon, the coastline is wilder and more rugged. Reclamation along the east coast, between Anse Etoile and the airport, makes this coast less interesting until south of the airport where there are beautiful beaches, most notably Anse Royale.

In the south, Intendance and Takamaka are spectacular beaches, though swimming can be dangerous from May to September. On the west coast, the best swimming is at Anse à la Mouche, sheltered by its wide sweeping corners all year round.

Rainfall in the mountains is double that at the coast, which can make mountain paths slippery, especially during December–February. If you wish to explore the hills, the best time is during the drier, less humid months, May–September.

Itinerary 1 takes you to the best beaches, viewing points, craft centres and the finest of the mountain passes, Sans Souci. This is followed by a selection of other itineraries which can be done without checking out of your Mahé hotel. Several of these options can be extended overnight or longer at your leisure.

A car is essential for the full day itinerary on Mahé, and useful for the capital city of Victoria and for the walking tours, though public transport can be used for these trips. Mahé's roads are good, but apart from the East Coast Highway, are narrow and winding. The Mini Moke is commonly used, although a closed car is more secure if you wish to lock away valuables while taking a dip or visiting sites.

1. From Bel Ombre to Beau Vallon

On this fairly leisurely full day, you will get to know the island and take in some spectacular scenery. We suggest a quick lunch, making the most of the daylight hours, and taking time over a more lavish dinner. Choose a weekday for your tour as many of the shops in this itinerary which sell crafts close on Sunday. You may wish to return to any of the scenic spots another day.

This tour sets out from Beau Vallon. If you are staying at the Coral Strand Hotel, or at another hotel north of this hotel, drive towards Victoria as far as Beau Vallon Police Station. Turn right here. If you are staying at Beau Vallon Bay Hotel or Fisherman's Cove, turn right

on leaving your hotel and you are on the correct road. From other parts of Mahé, head towards Beau Vallon Police Station and keep on the road towards Bel Ombre. Do not turn down to Beau Vallon Bay itself. If you are staying at any of the west coast hotels, drive north to do the Sans Souci-Beau Vallon section first.

Before setting out, call either **Jardin du Roi** (tel: 371313) or **Kaz Kreol Restaurant** (closed Monday, tel: 371680) to make lunch reservations, and any one of the recommended

Spices at Jardin du Roi

restaurants in the *Eating Out* section to reserve a table for dinner. Jardin du Roi is in a mountain setting, and Kaz Kreol on a sandy beach which is good for swimming. Jardin du Roi is not to be missed, with or without lunch, being one of the most interesting sites in Seychelles. Both are relaxed and informal.

Bel Ombre to Bel Air: After 1½km (1 mile) along the **Bel Ombre** road, you pass **Le Corsaire Restaurant** which offers upmarket din-

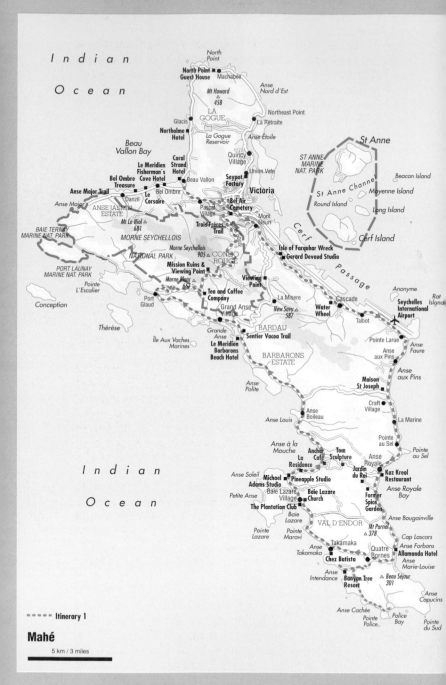

Indian

Ocean

North
Point

North Point
Guest House Machabée
Mt Howard
△
458
Anse
Nord d'Est
Glacis LA
GOGUE Northeast Point
Northolme La Retraite
Beau **Hotel** *La Gogue*
Vallon Bay *Reservoir* *Anse Étoile*
Coral Quincy
Le Meridien **Strand** Village
Fisherman's **Hotel** Union Vale
Cove Hotel Beau Vallon **Seypot**
Bel Ombre Bel Ombre **Factory**
Treasure **Victoria**
Anse Major Trail **Le** Pascal **Bel Air**
Danzil **Corsaire** Village **Cemetery**
Anse Major **ANSE JASMIN** Mont
ESTATE Fleuri
Mt Le Niol △
BAIE TERNAY 681
MARINE NAT. PARK **Trois Frères**
MORNE SEYCHELLOIS **Trail**
Morne Seychellois **Isle of Farquhar Wreck**
NATIONAL PARK 905 △ **CONGO** **Gerard Devoud Studio**
PORT LAUNAY **ROUGE**
MARINE NAT. PARK **Mission Ruins &**
Pointe **Viewing Point**
L'Escalier *Morne Blanc* △ **Viewing**
Conception 667 **Point**
Tea and Coffee La Misère Cascade
Company New Savy △
Thérèse **Grand Anse** 587 **Water** Talbot
Village **Wheel** **Seychelles**
Île Aux Vaches **BARDAU** **International**
Marines **Airport**
Grande **Sentier Vacoa Trail** Pointe Larue
Anse *Anse*
Le Meridien *Faure*
Barbarons *Anse*
Beach Hotel **BARBARONS** *aux Pins*
ESTATE **Maison**
Anse **St Joseph**
Polite **Craft**
Village
Anse La Marine
Anse Louis Boileau Pointe
Anse à la au Sel *Pointe*
Mouche **Anchor** **Tom** *au Sel*
La **Café** **Sculpture** *Anse*
Residence **Jardin** *Royale*
Anse Soleil **Michael** **Pineapple Studio** **du Roi** **Kaz Kreol**
Adams Studio Baie Lazare **Restaurant**
Petite Anse Village **Baie Lazare** *Anse Royale*
The Plantation Club **Church** **Former** *Bay*
Baie **Spice**
Pointe *Lazare* **Garden** *Anse Bougainville*
Lazare **VAL D'ENDOR** Mt Parnel
Pointe △ 378 *Cap Lascars*
Maravi *Anse Forbans*
Takamaka **Allamanda Hotel**
Anse Quatre *Anse*
Takamaka Bornes *Marie-Louise*
Chez Batista △ *Beau Séjour*
Anse 301 *Anse*
Intendance **Banyan Tree** *Capucins*
Resort
Anse Cachée
Pointe Police
Police *Bay* *Pointe*
du Sud

Indian

Ocean

St Anne

ST ANNE
MARINE
NAT. PARK *Beacon Island*
St Anne Channel *Moyenne Island*
Round Island *Long Island*

Cerf Island

Cerf

Passage

Anonyme

Rat
Island

- - - - **Itinerary 1**

Mahé

5 km / 3 miles

ing, (Tuesday–Sunday 7.30–10pm, closed Monday) on the right. With small boats anchored inside the breakwater protecting the attractive thatched restaurant building, this is a good place to stop for a photograph.

After a further 200m (220yds), you reach the fascinating site of Seychelles' most famous treasure dig at **Bel Ombre**. The 18th-century French pirate Olivier Le Vasseur was supposed to have buried

Bel Ombre pirate treasure dig

his share of the loot – gold and silver bars, strings of pearls, some 5,000 golden guineas, 42 diamonds and the jewel-encrusted regalia of the Archbishop of Goa, which included a large cross studded with rubies – from a Portuguese treasure ship somewhere in this area. Reginald Cruise-Wilkins, a former British big game hunter from Kenya, began the dig at Bel Ombre in the 1960s and his family steadfastly continue the search till today. It is believed that Le Vasseur laid out the site like a vast gaming board based on Greek mythology, and anyone in pursuit of his treasure has to perform the Twelve Labours of Hercules to reach it. The final step, a descent into the underworld, involved excavating an underwater cavern, which explains the sea walls and pumping equipment you can see on the site today.

Carry on to **La Scala Restaurant** (see *Eating Out*) where the road widens and it is easy to turn around and return the way you came. Pass the junction by the Beau Vallon Police Station and continue towards Victoria: there is a petrol station on your right. Chances are your hired car will be delivered to your hotel with an almost empty tank. As this is the last petrol station for a long while on this route, take the opportunity to fill up; 15 litres (3.3 gallons) will be enough.

You will be facing the conical mount of **Signal Hill**, where in the days before the airport opened, lookouts were posted to watch for approaching ships in the distance. Messengers would run down to Victoria with the news that mail and fresh supplies were on the way. After a series of bends, the road crosses the brow of the hill.

The capital **Victoria** and its port are spread before you. Continue

downhill in the direction of the town. Look out for the Hertz Car Hire sign on the right, just opposite **Kaz Zanana** *(see Itinerary 2)* on the left near the bottom of the hill, and take the next turning to the right, **Bel Air Road**.

A short distance along Bel

Hoarding in Victoria

Obelisk of the Seychelles 'Giant'

Air Road, where it bears to the right, is a bus stop on the left. Immediately after this is a wall with a gateway to the **Bel Air Cemetery**. This is a national monument, though rather overgrown and neglected now. Graves here date from the earliest settlement. Jean-François Hodoul, a corsair based in Seychelles who harried English shipping during the Napoleonic Wars is buried here, as is the so-called Seychelles 'Giant' – his grave said to be marked by an **obelisk**.

The giant, reputed to be nearly 3m (9ft) tall according to legend, is supposed to have been murdered by other settlers who were afraid of his great strength. Some graves are made from imported volcanic rocks from Mauritius, others of local beach rock.

Continue uphill, past **Thoughts Stained Glass Studio** on the left, where beautiful, though expensive, souvenirs are made and displayed. Shortly after this, take note of **Hotel Bel Air** on the right and look for a turning on the left; turn here into **Liberation Road**. Soon an excellent view of Victoria, the yacht basin, port and St Anne Marine Park opens up on your left. This is another good photographic stop. This back way around Victoria is worth remembering if you have to pass through town during rush hour, or on Saturday mornings when cars attempt to park where no space exists and a stream of pedestrians who cross the road choke up the one-way system. Continue to the next T-junction and turn right.

Victoria to Anse Royale: Continue to the next roundabout, known as **La Misère roundabout**, and turn right, heading up the hill. After 2km (1¼ miles), look out for a **view point** on the left

View of Victoria from Liberation Road

and turn into this lay-by. A ceramic signboard helps you to pick out the islands in the distance. The view encompasses the islands of St Anne Marine National Park, Praslin (on the horizon) and its satellites, and several other islands. The flat area spread out before you is reclaimed land, as is the airstrip to your right. The dramatic hillside to your right was made famous in a Tarzan film when our hero fell off this hill and discovered a lost world populated by African wild animals. Today, a brewery has been built at the base of this cliff. Return by the same route to the La Misère roundabout and turn right.

After ½km (¼ mile), look out for the rotting hulk of the **Isle of Farquhar** inter-island schooner, which now lies land-locked by the reclaimed land of the east coast, followed by the gallery of the French painter **Gerard Devoud** (Monday–Friday 8am–4pm, Saturday 8am–noon, closed Sunday and public holidays).

Continue on past Seychelles Breweries, Chelle Medical and the Kreol Or factory. **Kreol Or** manufactures quality jewellery and souvenirs, but to buy any of these you must visit one of their retail outlets in Victoria, on Praslin or La Digue.

Continuing southwards, immediately after the Cascade Telephone Exchange on the right, is Seychelles' only **water wheel**, now derelict. Built in 1910, its original purpose was to power coir and rope making machinery: today it turns for effect only. The rocks to the left of the water wheel are often draped in washing, the area being a sort of launderette for the locals. The church on the nearby hillside is one of the most photogenic in Seychelles. Turn right at the next T-junction, where there is an attractive water feature on the left, flowing over some typical Seychelles granite boulders.

Drive past the airport, past **Katiolo Restaurant and Discotheque** (see *Nightlife*), through Anse aux Pins village and past the Reef Hotel with the golf course just opposite the hotel. About 1km (½ mile) past the hotel is the Creole Institute (signposted Lenstiti Kreol) at **Maison St Joseph**. This is a lovely example of an old style Seychellois plantation house.

After a further 500m (550yds) is a sign indicating the **Craft Village** signposted **Val Des Prés Estate** and **Vye Marmit Restaurant** (Monday–Saturday 11am–11pm). Turn right here, and before visiting the craft village itself, park on the right to visit **Maison Coco**, which displays colourful crafts made from coconut products. There are shops at the craft village selling paintings – including originals by Liz Rouillon, Barbara Jenson and Colbert Nourrice –

T-shirts, beachwear, soaps, essential oils, colourful mobiles and so on. The craft village is open daily, mainly 9am–4pm, but only a few kiosks open on Sundays. It is also well worth visiting the **Plantation House** museum here. The restaurant serves excellent Kreol cuisine including delicacies such as fruit bat, octopus salad, crab curry and sausage fricasse with lentils.

Maison St Joseph

Craft Village store

Return to the main road and continue to **La Marine** (Monday–Friday 7.30am–5pm, Saturday 8am–3.30pm, closed Sunday and holidays), another model boat workshop. On the same site is the **Ecomusee La Plaine St Andre** (Tuesday–Friday 10am–5pm, Saturday–Sunday 1–5pm), a restored traditional planter's house furnished with colonial pieces.

Continue to the next village, **Anse Royale**. Opposite the petrol station is **Kaz Kreol Restaurant and Pizzeria** (open 11am–10pm). They have a large and varied menu to cater for every taste. The location is beautiful, the restaurant being right on the beach.

Alternatively, for lunch, continue southwards past Seychelles Polytechnic. Take the next turning on the right opposite a derelict church. This road is **Les Cannelles**. Continue for 850m (950yds) and turn left on to **Sweet-Escott Road**. Continue for a further 150m (165yds) and turn right on a single track road leading uphill. After a further 850m (950yds) you reach the **Jardin du Roi** (daily 10am–5.30pm). This lies close to the site of the **Royal Spice Garden**, where the French tried to grow spices in the early days of settlement, hoping to break the Dutch monopoly of these valuable commodities.

Jardin du Roi is a renovated plantation, specialising in growing spices including pepper, nutmeg, cinnamon, cloves and other crops traditional in Seychelles before the era of the great coconut plantations. There are several walks laid out through the grounds, and trees are identifiable from a leaflet given to

Granite outcrops at Anse Royale beach

visitors. The fascinating little museum, housed in the plantation house, has displays relating to Seychelles history, geology, stamps and the cultivation of spices. The restaurant menu is based on Kreol cuisine, with many imaginative innovations. The homemade ice cream, which includes a delicious cinnamon flavour, is excellent.

Anse Royale to West Coast: Whether you have dined at Jardin du Roi or just visited, return to Sweet-Escott Road and turn right. The road passes the site of the actual Royal Spice Garden, though this is now overgrown and forgotten. At the junction with the coast road, turn right, continue to **Anse Marie-Louise** and follow the road inland to **Quatre Bornes**. Here, opposite the police station, is a turning signposted to **Intendance**. This is a good and relatively secluded beach to visit but do not try to swim here unless it is calm, especially during April to October. If you have the slightest doubt, give it a miss. Turning left, follow the Intendance Road for about 1½km (1 mile) until you meet a turning to the right, signposted '**Banyan Tree**'. Take this turning, keep left at the Banyan Tree entrance and follow the track to the beach.

On returning to the junction, it is possible to follow the road southwards to even wilder pastures, past **Rosi's Little Jam Shop** where you can buy tasty home-made preserves. The road ends at a checkpoint for a military camp, and here you must double back. Return to Quatre Bornes and turn left at the police station, heading downhill to **Takamaka**. Though the beach at Takamaka is picturesque, there are dangerous currents here. **Chez Batista** (daily 9am–10pm), in the corner of the bay, is another excellent watering hole. The restaurant offers rather expensive Creole cuisine.

The road now bends northwards, rounding a rocky point (Pointe Maravi) to **Baie Lazare**. Just after the road turns to the left – to pass close by the sandy shore – is a monument which commemorates

the 250th anniversary of the first official French landing on Mahé by Lazare Picault in 1742.

Continue to the **Gérard Devoud's Art Studio**, opposite the turning to Plantation Club. On the hill is **Baie Lazare Church** at the northern end of the bay and another art studio, that of **Donald Adelaide** (daily 9am–6pm, closed Sunday).

Shortly after this, a turning to the left

Baie Lazare church

leads to **Anse Soleil**, a beautiful secluded beach, excellent for swimming and with a small beach-side restaurant. Descending to **Anse aux Poules Bleues**, the **Michael Adams Studio** is on the left (Monday– Friday 9am– 4pm, Saturday 9am–noon, closed Sunday and public holidays) which exhibits paintings by one of Seychelles' most celebrated artists, Michael Adams. A short distance further on is **Pineapple Studio**, which sells a whole range of original souvenirs.

Return to the coast road and continue northwards to the next bay, **Anse à la Mouche**. This is the perfect place for a swim when the tide is in; the bay is calm and sheltered at all times of year and never crowded. The **Anchor Cafe** (open daily 11am–10pm) serves snacks and drinks at good prices. Kayaks may be hired here, an excellent way to explore the calm waters of the bay.

Take the first turning to the right after Anchor Cafe, **Les Canelles Road**, and drive 800m (½ mile) to visit the studio of sculptor Tom Bowers, who makes limited edition high quality bronzes. This is on the right, the turning indicated by a signboard: '**Tom Sculpture Studio**'.

Return to the coastal road after your visit and turn right. After 8km (5 miles), immediately past Barbarons Hotel, there is a boardwalk through mangroves on the left and **Sentier Vacoa Trail** on the right. It is well worth a stop to explore this easy nature walk.

Carry on along the coastal road, past the BBC Indian Ocean Relay Station, ignoring the turning to the right near here. After a further 1½km (1 mile), you reach **Grande Anse**. This long sandy beach has been designated a Site of Outstanding Natural Beauty, but swimming here can be dangerous. Take the next major right-hand turning after a further 4km (2½ miles) in Port Glaud. This is the **Sans Souci Road**, marked by the Port Glaud Police Station on the right.

A Tom Bowers sculpture

Sans Souci to Beau Vallon: **Sans Souci** is the highest and most spectacular mountain pass, with the best views and a lush forest. Most of the road lies within the **Morne Seychellois National Park**. As the road winds upwards, the best spot for a photograph of the west coast is after 1.8km (1 mile).

Drive on a further 2½km (1½ miles) to **Seychelles Tea and Coffee Company** (Monday–Friday 9am–4pm, Saturday 8am–4pm). Guided tours are arranged according to demand (enquire at the kiosk). A short distance after the tea factory, note the signboard on the left, marking the start of the walk to the summit of **Morne Blanc** (see *Activities*). About 2½km (1½ miles) after the tea factory is another signboard for **Mission Historical Ruins and Viewing Point**. Turn left here and park at the top. It is well worth the visit for the view and the eerie silence lending atmosphere to a magnificent avenue of trees leading up to the viewing lodge. The ruins, dating from 1875, are that of a school built by missionaries to educate the children of liberated slaves in the last century.

Return to the Sans Souci Road, over the summit. Note the start of another walk, on the right-hand side to **Copolia**, followed about 1km (½ mile) later by another footpath signposted to **Trois Frères** to the left. About 1½km (1 mile) after the **Trois Frères Trail** sign, the road bends to the left and on the right are two white pillars marking a private driveway. This used to be the residence of the American ambassador until the embassy in Seychelles was closed down. During the 1950s, it was known as **The Lodge**, a mountain retreat for the British governor, and was chosen in 1956 to accommodate the exiled Archbishop Makarios of Cyprus. Continuing your descent, look out for a turning to the left signposted Curio Road. The turning is on a sharp bend to the right and the last landmark before it is **Rose Garden Restaurant**, 800m (880yds) prior to the turning. Take this turning. Brace yourself for a double hairpin bend even tighter than those on the Sans Souci Road. A short distance further on you will pass the Russian Embassy and reach a T-junction. Turn right, then left at the next T-junction soon after, returning to Beau Vallon and Bel Ombre via this route.

If you wish to continue to Victoria, ignore the turning to Curio Road, carrying on to the end of the Sans Souci Road. Turn right at the T-junction for the town centre. If in need of refreshments, turn left at the junction and look out for **Kaz Zanana** almost immediately on the right (see *Itinerary 2* for details).

Mission Ruins framed by sangdragon trees at Morne Seychellois National Park

2. Victoria and Botanical Gardens

Visit Victoria's Botanical Gardens to see the flora of the tropics. The capital city of Victoria is the heart of Seychelles, where past history and present culture can be sampled. Mornings are best; it is cooler, there is more produce in the market and the flora is at its best. Avoid Saturday – too crowded – and Sunday – just the opposite, almost everywhere is closed. A half day will cover this.

Drive to the Botanical Gardens (open daily 8am–6pm), or take a bus to Victoria (a signboard on the bus states the destination) and walk out of town along Francis Rachel Street. The gardens are situated on the Mont Fleuri Road, about 300m (1,000ft) after Le Chantier Roundabout (with a statue of a sailfish in the centre). The entrance is on the right just before the turning to the hospital, and the car park is located immediately to the right, inside the gate.

Pretty lily

There is a kiosk next to the car park where a useful leaflet to the gardens can be picked up. Walk uphill past an avenue of palms and ignore the next turning on the right. Just after this on the right is the indigenous coco de mer palm laden with its strange nuts. If you are not planning to visit the Vallée de Mai on Praslin where the coco de mer grows wild, step up for a closer look. Just behind is a pen full of giant land tortoises.

About 50m (165ft) further uphill, cut across the grassy area on your right where you'll see pools with water plants. Go behind the fenced pool and ascend the steps leading to a derelict building, once a restaurant. Bear left towards a concrete track and follow this to the car park of the Ministry of Environment. Behind the ministry building there is an **Orchid Garden**. After visiting the orchid garden, return to your car.

Exit the gardens, turn left onto the main road and take the first turning off Le Chantier roundabout. This is Francis Rachel Street, which used to be the coastal road before the land to your right was reclaimed. The National Library is the big building to your right. Beyond it you will see the Cable & Wireless Building on the left. Look out just before this for **Kenwyn House**, a traditional house owned by the company, set back from the road. A little further on the left, set well back, is Victoria's only **mosque**. Turn right just after this and park at the **Stadium Car Park**.

Set off on foot along **Francis Rachel Street** and turn left to

Entrance to the Botanical Gardens

Clock Tower

the **Craft Kiosks** to see the variety of wares on sale. Then return in the opposite direction towards the centre of Victoria. Just after the service station is a bust of Pierre Poivre, who fostered the idea of growing spices in Seychelles. Behind, and just beyond is the **Court House**, an elegant colonial-style building. Ahead is the **Clock Tower**, a replica of the one near Victoria Station in London. It was erected in 1903 to commemorate Seychelles' new status as a Crown Colony independent of Mauritius. Originally black, it has been painted silver.

Cross over the road to the Post Office side and walk straight on to **Albert Street**, past the main taxi stand. Behind the taxi stand is a grassy area called **Gordon Square**, which was formed from the rubble of a huge landslide in 1862 that claimed many lives. The next building is **Camion Hall**, a shopping arcade, mainly for local crafts (*see Shopping*). Continue to the end of Albert Street, cross over and turn the corner to the left into Oliver Maradan Street. Across this road, steps lead up to the

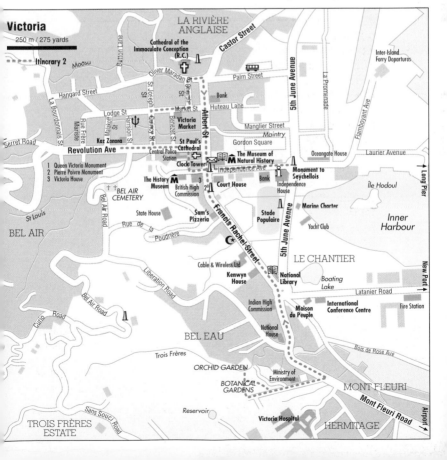

Victoria

250 m / 275 yards

Itinerary 2

LA RIVIÈRE ANGLAISE

Cathedral of the Immaculate Conception (R.C.)

Castor Street

Inter-Island Ferry Departures

Button Lane

Moosu

Oliver Maradan St

Palm Street

5th June Avenue

La Promenade

Hangard Street

St Joseph St

Ghanze St

Bank

Huteau Lane

Manglier Street

Flamboyant Ave

La Bourdonnais St

Rue Frère Mariste

Lodge St

Harrison St

Benezet St.

Clancy St

Market St

Victoria Market

Maintry

Gordon Square

Oceangate House

Laurier Avenue

Serret Road

Kaz Zanana

Central Police Station

St Paul's Cathedral

The Museum of Natural History

Revolution Ave

Clock Tower

Independence Ave

Monument to Seychellois

1 Queen Victoria Monument
2 Pierre Poivre Monument
3 Victoria House

BEL AIR CEMETERY

The History Museum

British High Commission

Court House

Bank

Independence House

Île Hodoul

St Louis

BEL AIR

Bel Air Road

State House

Rue de la Poudrière

Sam's Pizzeria

Francis Rachel Street

Stade Populaire

Marine Charter

Yacht Club

Inner Harbour

New Port

Liberation Road

Cable & Wireless Ltd

Kenwyn House

National Library

LE CHANTIER

Boating Lake

Latanier Road

Curio Road

Bel Air Road

Indian High Commission

Maison du Peuple

International Conference Centre

Fire Station

National House

BEL EAU

Trois Frères

ORCHID GARDEN

BOTANICAL GARDENS

Ministry of Environment

Bois de Rose Ave

MONT FLEURI

Sans Souci Road

Reservoir

Victoria Hospital

Mont Fleuri Road

Airport

TROIS FRÈRES ESTATE

HERMITAGE

Priests' Residence

right, into the grounds of the **Roman Catholic Cathedral**.

If you time your visit well and are here on the hour, you will hear the clock that chimes twice, made famous in the title of Alec Waugh's travel book, *Where The Clocks Chime Twice*. It is situated in a clock tower behind the cathedral. It chimes every hour, then again a few minutes later. Beyond the cathedral is the **Priest's Residence**, one of the most elegant buildings in Victoria.

Descend the cathedral steps, cross the road and go down **Church Street**. You cross a small river at this point. It is usually teeming with tilapia which the Seychellois do not eat, being spoilt for choice by the plethora of marine fish available. Turn right at the next junction into **Market Street**. The **Sir Selwyn Selwyn Clarke Market**, named after a former governor, is ahead to the left and right. The market was built in 1840. Renovation work along traditional architectural lines began in 1998 and the market was reopened in 1999. Enter the market and see the fish stalls to the left. Return to Market Street, turn left and walk to the end, about 100m (110yds). There is a small car park on your left, and across the road is Seychelles' only **Hindu Temple**.

At the junction of Market Street and **Quincy Street**, cross the road and turn left to the next T-junction. At this junction turn right and walk uphill for 150m (165yds) to **Kaz Zanana** (Monday to Saturday 9am–5.30pm, closed Sunday). This is a traditional wooden built house, one of the few surviving in Seychelles, and houses an art gallery featuring the work of George Camille and a café which serves the best cappucino and chocolate cake in Seychelles. From Kaz Zanana, return downhill, cross the road and continue on Revolution Avenue past the junction with Quincy Street for a further 100m (110yds). Take the alleyway between Central Police Station and the Anglican Cathedral. Behind these is another stream full of tilapia. Across the car park is **The Seychelles National Museum of History** (Monday to Friday 8.30am–4.30pm, Saturday 8.30am– noon, closed Sunday). There is a small entrance fee to be paid. The museum holds a miscellany of artefacts of historical interest housed in a very attractive balconied building in the colonial style.

From here, go down State House Avenue to the Clock Tower. Cross over a zebra crossing to the Court House, turn left and cross over to the **Post Office** on Independence Avenue. Immediately after the Post Office is **The National**

Selwyn Selwyn Clarke Market

Museum of Natural History (Monday to Friday 8.30am– 4.30pm, Saturday 8.30am–noon, closed Sunday). Again there is a small entrance fee. The museum includes displays of the flora and fauna of Seychelles and an excellent section dealing with the geological history of the islands. Across the road is another craft shop **Souvenir des Artisans des Seychelles**.

A little further on you will find Victoria's main watering hole, the **Pirates Arms**, just after Barclays Bank. Before calling in, it is worth continuing another 100m (110yds) to the **Tourism Information Office** at Independence House, where you can collect some reading material whilst you enjoy a snack and a cold drink. Return to the car park via the little road between Barclays and Pirates Arms and walk across the Pirates Arms car park to the Stadium car park.

3. St Anne and Baie Ternay Marine National Parks

See marine life on the coral reef through a subsea viewer without getting wet. Either a full-day trip with swimming, snorkelling and lunch on one of the islands of the St Anne Marine National Park (Moyenne, Round or Cerf) or a half-day trip with soft drinks only. If you prefer, opt for a tour of Baie Ternay Marine National Park, just off Mahe's west coast.

Glass bottom boat

Trips run daily: Mason's Travel (tel: 322642) runs trips exclusively to Moyenne; and Travel Services Seychelles (tel: 322414) to Cerf and Round. The trip cost also includes a transfer from your hotel to Marine Charter in Victoria and the park entrance fee. Pick-up time from west Mahé hotels and Glacis is at 8.15am, Coral Strand 8.30am, and other Beau Vallon hotels 8.40am. Arrive at Marine Charter at 9am, and after check-in, the glass bottom boat departs at 9.30am. Return to Mahé at around 4pm for the transfer back to your hotel. Creole Holidays (tel: 224900) arrange similar tours to Round island on Wednesdays and Cerf on Fridays and Saturdays. For tours to Baie Ternay, contact Teddy's Glass Bottom Boat (tel: 261125/511125), which runs daily from Coral Strand Hotel. Half-day trips depart at 2pm and return at 5pm. Full-day trips depart on Saturday at 10am.

The glass bottom boat affords a vertical view of the reef, but it also makes most fish scatter. The guide may amuse you by feeding sergeant major fish by hand, but it is also worth snorkelling to get a wider view of the reefs. The subsea viewer allows a horizontal view of the marine life, thereby scaring fewer fish. However, some find the enclosed nature of this type of vessel claustrophobic.

The islands of **St Anne Marine National Park** on the east are

An underwater symphony

easier to get to as there are more boats to the island. However, the coral has been heavily damaged through developments, including reclamation and coral bleaching caused by exceptionally high sea temperatures in 1998. **Round** island is tiny, and you can walk around it at a leisurely pace in 10 minutes. The beach is excellent for swimming. For a superb lunch, try **Chez Gabby**, the island's only restaurant. On **Moyenne**, owner Brendon Grimshaw has created a miniature botanical garden. Moyenne also provides a first-class lunch. **Cerf** is a much larger island, also with good swimming and more to explore. There are two good restaurants, the **Beach Shed**, where there are giant land tortoises, and the **Kapok Tree**.

The trip to **Baie Ternay Marine National Park** on the west is along a rocky coast looking up at the dramatic peak of Morne Seychellois. Full-day trips include a barbecue lunch at **Anse du Riz**. Apart from the extreme southeastern corner, this is the only stretch of Mahé with no coastal road. The soft corals of Baie Ternay have survived considerably better than those at St Anne's though it too has suffered some coral bleaching. For nature lovers, this option is the best in terms of the dramatic scenery both above and below water.

4. Scenic Flight

See Mahé and its satellite islands by helicopter. Only from this vantage point can you really take in the varied shades of the blue sea, the majestic green mountains and the beautiful beaches all at once. The flight lasts 15, 30 or 45 minutes, depending on your choice.

Scenic flights depart from Mahé's Domestic Terminal or from the Plantation Club. The flights also depart from other points around the island, so it is best to enquire with a travel agent or call Helicopter Seychelles (tel: 373900).

There are four seats, one next to the pilot and three just behind. The best seats for photography are by either window at the back. These windows have a slot which slides open to enable you to take photographs unimpeded. The co-pilot's seat has a smaller sliding window that photographers may find difficult to crouch down to, but the all-round view is superb for non-photographers. If you have an autofocus camera, you may find that the wind rushing past will play havoc with your controls if you poke the lens too far out. Take care that your spectacles or sunglasses don't get blown away.

From Mahé's Domestic Terminal, you take off and head towards the green velvet islands of St Anne Marine National Park. The flat land of the east coast of Mahé to your left was reclaimed during the 1980s and 1990s. Here you pass the industrial area of Providence followed by the Unity Stadium, which is used for all manner of sporting occasions.

Heading out to sea, the first major island is Cerf, surrounded by the smaller islands of Round and Moyenne, which are popular with day-trippers, and Long Island, which houses Seychelles' main prison. Beyond is St Anne, with its five-star St Anne Resort facing the busy port of Victoria.

Up, up and away!

Next you head northwards around the tip of the island and along the west coast to Beau Vallon. Leaving Seychelles' main tourist beach behind, there are glorious views of Mahé's wild side, including Morne Seychellois National Park, the solid greenery broken only by the granite slopes of Morne Blanc. On a 30-minute flight, you continue southward to near the Plantation Club before cutting across the island to return. A 45-minute flight will take you to the wild shores that fringe the south of Mahé and the beautiful bays of Takamaka and Intendance. Your whistle-stop tour is over in a flash, but you won't forget it for a long time.

Scenic flights also run from La Digue (on most days), following the coastlines of La Digue and Praslin, passing the islands of Félicité, Grande Seur, Petite Soeur, Curieuse, Cousin and Cousine. Though based at La Digue, trips can be also arranged from Praslin.

West coast of Mahé from the air

Spend a day visiting a beautiful volcanic island with no roads. The old way of plantation life still continues on Silhouette – the third largest island after Mahé and Praslin.

There is a small expensive hotel on Silhouette, the Silhouette Island Lodge (see page 89), 19km (12 miles) northwest of Mahé, but day trips by boat are possible. Make arrangements with Jimmy Mancienne (mobile tel: 510269), whose shop is just next to the Boat House restaurant on Beau Vallon. These trips cater for small parties and offer flexibility if arrangements are discussed in advance with Mancienne. Trips depart at 9am and return at 5pm.

La Passe jetty at Silhouette

Wear your swimsuit or shorts and shoes you can slip off easily. Flip flops are easy to slip on and off and are adequate for walking ashore, unless you plan any major ascents of Silhouette's steep mountains. There is some shade on the boat but take along sun screen and a hat. Soft drinks are available on the boat – included in the cost of the trip – as is the use of fishing gear, the landing fee for Silhouette and a barbecue lunch.

This day trip is flexible and usually includes trawl fishing if customers are interested. If you prefer to simply get to the islands and spend as much time ashore as possible, discuss this first with Mancienne and he will try to team you up with others of like mind, rather than a group of ardent fishermen. Landings are usually made only on **Silhouette**, the boat making a very interesting circuit around the coast of **North**, or anchoring off North for a spot of snorkelling. North Island is closed to day-trippers as it is reserved for guests of the only resort on the island, the **North Island Lodge** (tel: 293100). If you wish to visit **La Passe** on Silhouette, discuss this in advance with Mancienne so that he can obtain the requisite permission.

Beachside house, Silhouette

Assuming you do not spend too much time fishing, you will arrive at Silhouette by about 11am. You disembark onto a dinghy to be ferried ashore to a stone jetty at La Passe. There should be time to explore a little before lunch.

Set back from the beach is a lovely **plantation house**, now empty though well

Swaying palms and limpid waters – North Island view from Silhouette

maintained. This is the house of the wealthy Dauban family who used to own Silhouette till about 1983.

Follow the track to the left to the small group of wooden houses. On the right is an old *kalorifer*, where coconuts were dried to make copra. Nearby is the headquarters of **Nature Protection Trust of Seychelles**. The chairman of the trust, Ron Gerlach, gives talks at the **Visitors' Centre**, and conducts guided tours of their tortoise and terrapin conservation projects. The tortoises are believed to be survivors of the granitic island species, thought extinct until their rediscovery in the 1990s. The track climbs upwards through a gate and around a marsh to the right, which is now planted as a garden area. Beyond, framed

The Dauban Mausoleum

by tall coconut palms, is Seychelles' strangest monument, the **Dauban Mausoleum** – built to resemble a small Greek temple.

Continue over the hill and descend to the shore to **Anse Cimitière** and immediately beyond that to **Anse Lascars**. As you descend, there is a spectacular slope of volcanic syenite to your right. At the far side of Anse Lascars, at the top of the beach, are graves which are said to be Arabic in origin. Just beyond this beach is **Pointe Zeng Zeng**, the only place in Seychelles where black volcanic cinders can clearly be seen. Return to La Passe for your barbecue lunch by the beach. If you are not visiting La Passe, the barbecue is staged at **Anse Mondon**.

Silhouette rises to 740m (2,400ft), though 65 million years ago it was an enormous volcano rising to about 3,000m (10,000ft). The high forest contains many of Seychelles' unique plants, but to reach the best areas requires a long and sometimes difficult walk. There is an easier track which goes over a low pass in the hills. The starting point of this track is behind the houses to the right of the jetty. If feeling energetic, this walk will give you some idea of Silhouette's interior, but don't expect to conquer the summit in an afternoon. Take it easy, and allow yourself plenty of time to get back.

Alternatively, take a stroll along the beach to **Anse la Passe**, but keep clear of the hotel compound about 500m (550yds) north of the jetty as this is for hotel guests only.

Although it is not possible to land on North unless staying at the island's hotel, the sail around North is fascinating. The colours of the rocks (North is composed of syenite like Silhouette), the high ledges where endemic screwpines grow, the spectacular cliffs falling away into the sea and the caves eked out over centuries by the crashing of the waves are breathtaking. There is a lovely beach in the centre of each side of the island, once a thriving plantation.

You will probably linger ashore as long as possible, unless the main object of your trip was the fishing, so the best plan is to leave Silhouette at around 3.30pm to arrive back at Beau Vallon about 5pm, or leave 30 minutes earlier if taking the detour around North.

6. Anonyme Island

A day or half-day trip to Anonyme is an opportunity to enjoy a few hours at leisure. Timings are flexible; you can be as active, or idle as you choose, making use of watersports on offer or just relaxing by the pool.

This can be day or half-day trip. Call Anonyme Island Resort (tel: 380100 or mobile: 710111) and explain what you would like to do, arranging the time you wish to be transferred by boat.

You will need to drive or take a taxi to the Anonyme jetty, on re-claimed land just north of the airport. The boat crossing takes a few minutes across calm, sheltered waters.

On the island, there is a swimming pool, nice beaches for swimming (though the water is shallow at low tide) and a nature trail around the island. Snorkelling equipment is available, as are kayaks. It is usually possible to kayak to nearby deserted **Rat Island** in about 30 minutes but ask the staff for advice on conditions that day. The staff can direct you to the best spots for snorkelling. Diving or fishing trips can be arranged if discussed in advance.

Have a delicious lunch at the **Piment Vert** restaurant at the resort, or book a table for dinner if you decide to stay late. As with everything else, meal times are entirely flexible to suit your whim. If flying out of Mahé in the evening, you can be taken straight to the check-in desks at the airport by boat — something of a novelty if you live in a city.

Approaching Anonyme Island

PRASLIN

Praslin, though the second largest island of Seychelles with an area of 27½sq km (10½sq miles), is a big step back in time from Mahé. Life moves at a quieter, slower pace, but the hotels are as good. There are two main centres for tourists: one on the west coast at Grand Anse (just south of the airport which links the island to Mahé), and the other at Anse Volbert, on the opposite side.

Praslin's beaches are even better than Mahé's, with the southern section from Grand Anse to Baie Ste Anne by far the best. This section has some accommodation, but is largely undeveloped, unspoilt and picturesque.

Baie St Anne, in the southeast corner, is a natural sheltered harbour. Here, the ferries depart and arrive daily, linking Praslin with the islands of Mahé and La Digue *(see Practical Information)*.

The jewel of Praslin is the World Heritage Site of the Vallée de Mai, which lies within the Praslin National Park. A pilgrimage to this unique palm forest, where the strange coco de mer grows, is included in *Itinerary 7*. The island tour is best done by car – or better yet, by jeep – if it is to be completed in a day. Most roads are good, though the narrow roads to some of the more out of the way places are rather bumpy. Check the brakes before you set off, as rental cars are not always in the best of condition.

Boat trips from Praslin are the best way to see La Digue and the smaller satellite islands of Praslin, including Cousin and Curieuse,

Praslin's shores are blessed with beautiful beaches

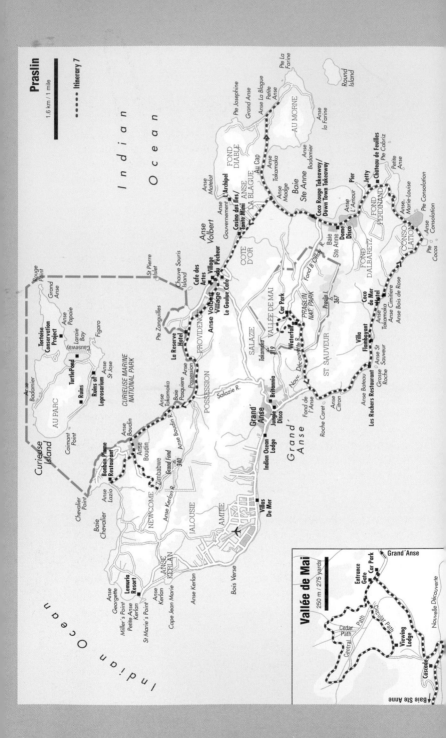

Praslin

1.6 km / 1 mile

····· Itinerary 7

Indian Ocean

Indian Ocean

Curieuse Island

Grand Anse
Rouge Point

Tortoise Conservation Project

Anse Papaie
Lazarie Bay
Figaro

Causeway
Turtle Pond
Anse St Jose
Ruins
Ruins of Leprosarium
Anse Badamier

AU PARC
Caiman Point

CURIEUSE MARINE NATIONAL PARK

Baie Chevalier
Chevalier Point
Anse Lazio
Anse Boudin

Ptc Rouge Point
St Pierre Islet
Chauve Souris Island

Ptc Zanguilles

Anse Matelot
Anse Gouvernement
Casino des Îles/ Gaîté Mimi
Archipel
ANSE LA BLAGUE

Ptc La Farine
Grand Anse
Anse La Blague
Petite Anse
Ptc Josephine

AU MORNE
Round Island

Au Cap
Anse Takamaka
Anse Madge
Cafe des Artes
Village du Pêcheur
La Goulue Cafe

ANSE VOLBERT
COTE D'OR

Baie Ste Anne
Anse Volbert Village

Baie Ste Anne

Anse Farine
FOND DIABLE

Anse Bois de Rose
Anse Cimitiere
Anse Takamaka
Coco de Mer Hotel

Anse La Blague

Anse Consolation
Ptc Consolation
Château de Feuilles
Ptc Cabriz
Petite Anse

Pier
Jetty
Coco Rouge Takeaway/ Down Town Takeaway
Anse L'Amour

FOND FERDINAND

Anse Marie-Louise

Dome Disco

FOND DALBARETZ

Anse Marie-Louise
Ptc Marie-Louise
CONSO LATION
Ptc Cocos
Anse Consolation

Anse Takamaka
La Reserve Hotel
Baie Possession
Anse Possession

PROVIDENCE
POSSESSION

SALAZIE
Salazie R.
Takamaka

NEWCOME
Anse Boudin
Bonbon Plume Restaurant
Anse Boudin R.
Anse Boudin
Zimbabwe
Grand Fond 340

VALLÉE DE MAI
Car Park
Waterfall
PRASLIN NAT. PARK
Praslin I. 367
ST SAUVEUR

Villa Flamboyant
Anse St Sauveur
Grosse Roche
Les Rochers Restaurant
Anse Bateau

Nou. Découverte R.
Anse Citron
Roche Caret
Fond de l'Anse

Grand' Anse
Jungle Disco
Britannia

Indian Ocean Lodge
Grand' Anse

JALOUSIE
AMITIE
Villas De Mer
Bois Verse

Anse Kerlan R.
ANSE KERLAN
Anse Kerlan
Lemuria Resort
Anse Georgette
Miller's Point
Petite Anse Kerlan
St Marie's Point
Cape Jean Marie
St Marie's Point
Anse Kerlan

Indian Ocean

Vallée de Mai

250 m / 275 yards

Grand' Anse
Entrance Gate
Car Park
Central Path
Cedar Path
Viewing Lodge
Nouvelle Découverte
Cascade
Baie Ste Anne

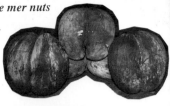

Coco de mer nuts

and a little further afield, the best preserved island and finest nature reserve of the granitic islands, Aride. All these are covered as day trips in *Itineraries 8–11*, several of which can be extended overnight.

7. Vallée de Mai to Anse Lazio

Visit the Vallée de Mai National Park to see the unique palm forest and the black parrot, Seychelles' national bird; then take the most beautiful coastal drive in Seychelles. A fairly busy morning and relatively lazy afternoon. You may wish to re-visit some of the beaches on another day.

To reach the starting point from Grand Anse or Praslin Airport, drive south (turn left at the junction of the airport road). Beyond the village, the main road turns left, uphill and inland. The Vallée de Mai is 2km (1¼ miles) up the hill. From Anse Volbert, drive south to Baie Ste Anne and turn right at the only junction with a major road, just after Barclays Bank. From Anse St Sauveur, drive north towards Grand Anse and take the first turning on the right. Fill up at Grand Anse or Baie Ste Anne Service Station (10 litres will be sufficient).

Park at the **Vallée de Mai** car park and purchase your entry ticket to the park (daily 7.30am–5.30pm) from the kiosk. It is also well worth buying the booklet *Vallée de Mai* by Katy Beaver and Lindsay Chong Seng. The wealth of information will add to your appreciation of this magnificent forest. Arrive early if you can. It is cool in the forest for most of the day, but the atmosphere is better enjoyed before the larger tourist groups arrive at mid-morning.

There is an **Information Centre** with souvenirs, snacks and drinks on sale. It is worth taking at least something to drink with you. Fruit juices in cartons are lightest, but don't forget to dispose of the emptied containers properly.

Young coco de mer plants

The paths in the park are well-marked but are unpaved, uneven and have some steep steps. Climb the steps to the right of the car park entrance. From the entrance, follow the numbered trail. It is worth doing the whole **Circular Path** at a leisurely pace, allowing 2 or 3 hours for the walk.

There are numerous young coco de mer trees at the start of the trail. There are separate male and female trees but at this age it is impossible to tell them apart. Its leaf petiole is the largest of any plant in the world but it is the double coconut from the female tree, the world's largest seed, that has made the tree famous. It is the shape – suggestive of the female pelvis – together with the equally suggestive shape of the male catkin that fascinates many non-botanists.

You will see mature male and female trees further into the valley; information boards dotted throughout the valley draw attention to these and other plants. It takes about 15 years before a trunk develops and another 20–40 years before the tree reaches maturity while the nuts take seven years to develop. Trees may live for over 200 years, some reaching some 32m (104ft) in height; males being much taller than females. Nuts may weigh 20kg (44lbs) and a tree can bear up to 35 nuts at a time, weighing up to an incredible 700kg (1540lbs) in total.

The British general, Charles Gordon, who is famous for his dramatic death during the defence of Khartoum, visited Seychelles in 1881 and was deeply impressed by the Vallée de Mai. He was a religious man and a serious thinker, and concluded that Seychelles was the actual site of the legendary Garden of Eden. He went on to write a lengthy treatise on the subject, in which he proposed that the coco de mer was the Tree of Knowledge, and the breadfruit the Tree of Life.

The Vallée de Mai has examples of all six palms unique to Seychelles scattered throughout the area, all of which are highlighted on the information boards. Apart from palms, the Vallée de Mai is also famous as the home of the Seychelles black parrot. You may hear their whistles almost anywhere but not see the birds because of the dense vegetation. The best places to look for these elusive parrots are near the entrance, along the roadside and from the northern viewpoint, where there is a shelter and benches to rest on. This is a good place to take a break and keep your eyes peeled open. Return to the car park via the Circular Path.

Vallée de Mai to **Anse Lazio**: From the car park, turn right and head towards **Grand Anse**. In just under 1km (½ mile), there is a

Another postcard pretty beach, this one at Anse Takamaka

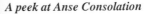

A peek at Anse Consolation

lovely waterfall framed by endemic palms on the right. At the bottom of the hill, turn left (signposted '**Anse Consolation**'). From this point to Baie Ste Anne, we think, is the most beautiful coastal car drive in Seychelles. There are eight bays, each one extremely photogenic.

First is **Anse Citron**, then **Anse Batcau**, at the far end of which is **Les Rochers Restaurant** (see *Eating Out*). Another 750m (825yds) further on the right is **Villa Flamboyant**, the lovely building surrounded by flame trees. There is a small art gallery here, well worth a visit, while the grounds of this guesthouse are an excellent site to see black parrots, especially in the late afternoon or early morning.

Beyond this point is **Anse Takamaka**, then **Anse Cimitiére** on the point of which is the **Black Parrot Hotel**. All these bays are good for a swim, though you may have to wade quite far out at low tide. Rounding **Pointe Cocos**, Anse Consolation is less ideal for swimming, due to the beach rock barrier here. The rock, which looks like fossilised coral, is formed where fresh river water mixes with sea water, causing calcareous materials to solidify.

Around **Pointe Consolation** is **Anse Marie Louise**, the best beach on this stretch of coast for a swim and a particularly quiet and picturesque spot to laze on the sands and soak up the sun. From the beach, the road winds steeply upwards to round **Point Cabriz** before descending equally steeply to Baie Ste Anne. The area to the left is **Fond Ferdinand**, a mainly coco de mer forest.

Turn left at the T-junction, pass the boat yard to your right and service station on the left; continue past the post office, market, community centre and ignore the major left turning (back to the Vallée de Mai). Just beyond this junction on the left are two cheap and cheerful takeaways, **Coco Rouge** (daily 10am–4pm, 6–10pm) and **Downtown** (daily 11am–2pm,

Building a boat

6–10pm) – perfect for a takeaway picnic lunch. You waste as little time as possible if you lunch this way, and the food is good and very cheap. If you do decide to do this, drive on out of the village, about 1km (½ mile), to **Anse Madge**. There is a gap between the trees where you can pull right off the road and park. You can either enjoy your picnic lunch here, or on the very peaceful beach which overlooks **Baie Ste Anne** to the right. There are no bins provided, so make sure that you take your litter home with you.

Continue on the coastal road. Where this road turns left inland

Casino des Iles

is a track going straight on to **Anse La Blague**. This is an interesting diversion to make. If you take this there-and-back trip, take the hills in first gear. Notice how pink the granite is here. Praslin is famous for this and some Mahé buildings, such as the Maison du Peuple (the parliament of Seychelles), are constructed from this pink granite; its colour caused by the presence of alkaline felspars. At Anse La Blague is **La Vanille Beach Bar** and a dive centre. The beach is an excellent spot for snorkelling.

Return to the main road and continue in the same direction (signposted '**Anse Boudin** 6km'). The road passes through pleasant takamaka and casuarina woodland. Soon you reach **Tante Mimi Coffee House and Restaurant** and **Casino des Iles**. The coffee house serves snacks, light meals, excellent ice cream and good coffee during the daytime. The excellent restaurant and casino is open on evenings only (see *Eating Out*).

A short distance further on, the road turns inland at the Mauritius Commercial Bank building. The road to the right of the bank is a cul de sac, but well worth a diversion to visit the **Cote D'Or Souvenir Boutique** next to the beach and **Galerie des Artes**, which is reached by parking at the end of this short road and continuing on foot along the coastal path.

Continue northwards on the Anse Boudin road, round Pointe Zanguilles and past the turning to the La Reserve Hotel, emerging back on the coast at **Anse Possession**, where the French staked their claim to the island in 1768. The lead plaque they had laid disappeared within a few years and it was suspected the English had taken it. There was a rumour that it had been tampered with by an officer of an English ship who replaced the name of the French ship with that of his own.

The coast north of here, facing Curieuse Island, is very pretty, quiet, and good for swimming. At Anse Boudin, the road turns inland and after a short distance there is a signpost on the left to **Zimbabwe**. Take this winding road which leads to a magnificent viewing point across to Mahe in the west, Curieuse in the east and Aride Island to the north. Return to the junction and turn left to **Anse Lazio**.

Anse Lazio is one of the most popular beaches on Praslin and has been voted the best beach in the world in a number of surveys by international travel magazines. It is excellent for swimming except in rough weather. The nearby **Bon Bon Plume Restaurant** (daily, lunch only), sells mainly seafood and is fairly expensive. Backtrack from here to your hotel when you've had enough of this lovely beach.

8. La Digue

Possibly the most beautiful granite island of Seychelles, the spectacular La Digue coast – with its huge boulders towering over perfect beaches – is backdrop to many a glossy magazine advertisement. You will need a whole day on La Digue for this cycling tour.

As there is no airstrip on La Digue, take a 30-minute ride on the ferry to the island from Baie Ste Anne jetty on Praslin. Call the Inter-Island Ferry Service (tel: 232329) beforehand, and book yourself on the 9am ferry. There are also departures at other times and comfortable accommodation on the island if you decide to spend the night (see Practical Information). If you do not have a car, ask your hotel to arrange a taxi to the Baie Ste Anne jetty – allow 30 minutes from Grand Anse and 15 minutes from Anse Volbert. Ask the taxi driver to pick you up on your return on the 5.45pm ferry – arriving on Baie Ste Anne at 6.15pm – since taxis do not always meet the ferries.

As there are few vehicles on La Digue, the third largest island at 10sq km (4sq miles), the best way to see it is by bicycle *(see next page)*. The roads are paved and even, making cycling easy even for the most nervous of riders. It is possible to do the tour on foot if

you are a brisk walker, or you can hire one of just three taxis on the island. Ox cart rides are a novelty but can be tediously slow.

There are restaurants and a café on La Digue, as well as shops where you can buy snacks: so unless you prefer to take a packed lunch from your hotel, you need not worry about food until you get there. You arrive at **La Passe** jetty, near the same point where **La Digue**'s first settlers arrived.

These people were exiled from the Indian Ocean island of Bourbon — now Reunion — after leading a rebellion because they thought the French governors were going to hand Bourbon over to the British. The French plan was to exile the rebels on the Indian coast, but instead, the rebels hijacked the ship and forced the captain to bring them to La Digue.

Up to that point, the island had not been successfully settled, perhaps because of the difficult landing. These exiles stuck it out however, and La Digue became one of the most prosperous islands of all, studded with rich plantations. Today, a small and friendly local population live on the land, thriving on fishing or by boat-building. Old planters' houses and a sleepy pace of life add to the charm.

Arrival at La Passe

When you arrive, note the **Tarosa Café** (daily 10.30am–6.30pm) on the right-hand side at the end of the jetty. You may wish to return here later for an inexpensive lunch. There is a useful **Tourist Information Office** on the right (Monday–Saturday 8am–5pm, Sunday 9am–noon). There will probably be ox carts waiting to meet tourists booked on a package trip. Ox carts were once the main form of public transport on La Digue, but today there are a couple of buses and an increasing number of pick-up trucks on the island. These days, ox carts are retained just for the tourists.

You will also see plenty of bicycles for hire in this vicinity. Make sure you feel comfortable with the bike you hire and that the brakes work well. On foot, or by bike, set off heading south (turn right on leaving the jetty). Looking out to sea, there is a good view of the

BICYCLES FOR HIRE

La Digue Cross. This monument was erected on top of granite rocks in the bay in 1931 by Swiss priest Georges Fuffeieux, in memory of people who drowned while attempting to land on La Digue in the past.

A short distance further on the right is the **Logan Hospital**, named after a former British governor of Seychelles. There are a number of traditional houses in this vicin-

La Digue's eco-friendly transport

Lunch under swaying palms at the Tarosa Café

ity; two are situated on the right just after **Choppy's Bungalows** (tel: 234224), where relatively inexpensive accommodation can be found.

At the more expensive **La Digue Island Lodge** (tel: 234232), the road turns left inland and then right, passing behind the hotel to a T-junction. Turn left and after about 100m (328ft) you reach the **Flycatcher Reserve** on the right. The reserve was initially established by Christopher Cadbury, the chocolate industrialist and nature conservationist, who rented this area of forest from the land owner to preserve one of the best habitats for the Seychelles black paradise flycatcher. Later, the area was acquired by the Seychelles government and given legal protection.

The best way to see the flycatcher is to walk along the trails beneath the trees to the far side of the reserve – a point soon reached as the reserve is long but narrow. The male fly-catcher is probably the most beautiful of Seychelles' unique birds. Its long black tail gives the bird its local name, *vev*, meaning widow, because of its 'widow's weeds'.

Flycatcher Reserve

The flycatchers are almost entirely confined to La Digue – there are just a few birds on Félicité – with a population here of about 200. There is tremendous pressure on their habitat from the growing human population and the boat-building industry, but at least local boys have dropped the habit of killing them for sport – thanks to the interest tourists take in La Digue's special bird.

On the opposite side of the road to the reserve is **Zerof Restaurant and Take-Away** (daily 11.30am–9.30pm), an excellent spot for lunch. Continue inland and turn left at the sign for **Belle Vue** (2½km/1½ miles). About 200m (220yds) further on you pass **Chateau St Cloud** to your right. Built at the height of Napoleon's

Chateau St Cloud sign

empire, and named after the small French town St Cloud, south of Paris, the chateau was once part of a vanilla farm and remnants of the old vanilla factory can still be seen nearby.

Continue to follow the same road which arches back to rejoin the coastal road near the jetty. Buy a refreshing drink from one of the local shops or the Tarosa Café which sells fresh fruit juices.

Head north along the coastal road. It turns inland to round Cap Barbi and then descends to **Anse Sévère**. Around the next point is **Anse Patates**, the location of **Patatran Restaurant**. You might like to return here for a delicious and moderately-priced Creole lunch. The location is superb, sheltered from prevailing winds which may blow from the northwest or the southeast. It is also an excellent spot for a bit of swimming and snorkelling.

Continue around the point of land jutting out into the sea and you reach a wild stretch of coast. In places, wind-blown sand may make cycling difficult. If you see a patch of sand ahead, it is better to disembark; you could be sent flying over the handlebars (we speak from personal experience!). The first bay is **Anse Gaulettes**, a long bay of almost 1km (½ mile), followed by smaller bays, half this size, of **Anse Grosse Roche**, **Anse Banane**, and **Anse Fourmis**, where the track finally peters out. There is a footpath that continues around the next corner, but it is not suitable for bicycles. Turn around and return to Patatran or Tarosa for lunch.

Once refreshed, return southwards and turn right at the T-junction behind La Digue Island Lodge. At the coast, turn left to **L'Union Estate**. Before reaching the estate, visit **Green Gecko Gallery** (Monday–Friday 9am–5pm, Saturday 9am–noon, closed Sunday) and **Barbara Jenson Studio** (daily 8am–6pm). Just before L'Union Estate is a small **cemetery** to the right, by the sea, which is worth a look. Buried here are some of the earliest settlers on La Digue.

There is a small charge for entering L'Union Estate which produces high grade copra (dried coconut). There is a *kalorifer* for drying the coconut flesh and an oil press – a kind of giant mortar and pestle. The oil is used for various purposes, including cooking and the manufacture of soap, hair oil and suntan lotion.

Vanilla is also grown here. It was a lucrative crop on La Digue following its introduction around 1866 but the industry crashed about half a century later, mainly due to the development of cheaper synthetic vanillin.

Other attractions of L'Union Estate include the huge **La Digue**

A bullish ride on La Digue

Rock and a few tame giant land tortoises. There is also a **plantation house** which has earned its place in history because one of the infamous soft porn *Emmanuelle* films was made in its premises in the early 1990s. Follow the road past these various sites until it curls back towards the beach at **Anse Union** and **Pointe Source d'Argent**. With the sun high in the sky, this could be a good time to simply relax and enjoy a siesta under the shade.

A harvest of coconuts

La Digue's plantation house

Thus revitalised, exit from the estate and take the sharp turning to the right, signposted for **Grand Anse**. The land on either side of the road soon becomes quite marshy. The area is known as **La Mare Soupape**. *Soupap* is the local word for terrapin, and many of these unique Seychelles creatures can be found here.

Just beyond the marsh, the road bends sharply to the left. The group of dramatic granite rocks immediately on the right at this point are worth a second glance, or maybe even a photograph. At a height of nearly 3m (10ft) above the ground, look for a wedge of fossilised beach rock, indicating that the sea level was once higher than it is today.

Just before the road turns uphill, there is a glimpse of the **Grand Anse River**. This is a local launderette of sorts where the women gather to wash their clothes in the river and lay them out on the ground to dry.

Eventually the road heads downhill, with large trees giving some shade. When you reach the beach, however, there is less shade. It can be dangerous to swim here during May–October. Allow about an hour for a leisurely journey back to La Passe for your ferry home – a distance of nearly 5km (3 miles).

9. Aride

Leased and managed by the Island Conservation Society (ICS), the 68-ha (168-acre) Aride is the finest nature reserve of the granitic Seychelles and a conservationist's paradise. It has more breeding species of seabirds than the other 38 granite islands combined, plants found nowhere else on earth and rare endemic land birds. A full-day trip from Praslin.

Contact your hotel reception for details of trips. Not all hotels arrange trips to Aride, and if this approach fails, call Mason's Travel, Praslin (tel: 233211); Travel Services Seychelles, Praslin (tel:

Landing on Aride

233438); Louis Bedier, Praslin (tel: 232192); or Dream Yacht (tel: 232681). The cost of your trip includes lunch and a landing fee payable to ICS. If booked through a travel agent, the trip may also include a transfer from your hotel to the boat departure point, which varies depending on which boat you are going on.

Aride has no jetty, so visiting boats moor offshore and transfer passengers to the island's small boats. Getting ashore calls for visitors to be nimble in disembarking. The island paths are steep, uneven and exposed to the sun in parts, so exercise care.

Weather conditions sometimes make landings difficult. It is best to plan a visit to Aride as early as possible during your stay; if weather conditions are unfavourable, you can reschedule your trip. The island is open to visitors only three days a week: Monday, Wednesday and Sunday. If you wish to check in advance on landing conditions, call the island's warden at tel: 321600. You should wear shorts or a bathing costume and carry your shoes, as it will be a wet landing on the beach. Cameras, towels and valuables should be carried in a plastic bag as they may be splashed, especially when leaving and heading into the swell.

You should take binoculars if you have one, a sun hat, sun cream and walking shoes (not flip flops as the hill path is rocky and rough). A bottle of water or soft drinks for the hill walk are also useful, but do not weigh yourself down. Soft drinks are provided with lunch by most of the boats which arrange trips to Aride. Bring your own towel, and if you like, snorkelling equipment. Photographers should take plenty of film as both scenery and birds are very photogenic. Lunch is provided on organised trips, otherwise there is no food available on the island.

On arrival, you will transfer to a rigid hull inflatable or a fibreglass boat. Once ashore, a member of staff will point you in the direction of the **visitors' shelter** along the beach. When everyone is assembled and has put on their shoes, a guided tour departs from here. Although visitors are allowed to walk alone along the paths of the plateau, they should not climb the hill unescorted. The hillside is riddled with the burrows of wedge-tailed shearwaters, and much damage may be done to both bird and man if visitors wander at will in the forest. At certain times of the year, it is impossible to take tours up the hill because there are so many birds that visitors would cause great disturbance; birds, chicks and eggs could be trodden upon. Tours are done in English, though leaflets are also available in French, German and Italian.

From the visitors' shelter, a path cuts through coconut scrub to the coastal forest where you are likely to see one of the island's rarities, the Seychelles warbler. Once almost extinct and confined to Cousin, 29 birds were transferred to Aride in September 1988. Today, there are over 3,000 birds and the species has been taken off the Red Data list of endangered birds.

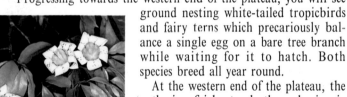

A noddy guarding its egg

From March to November you will see large numbers of lesser noddies and sooty terns. At the peak of the breeding season, the excited cries of the birds make Aride a very noisy place indeed. In addition, Aride has the world's largest colony of lesser noddies and the world's only hilltop colony of sooty terns. Roseate terns arrive around the end of April and depart at the end of August. It is interesting to know that Aride is their last remaining breeding site in the region.

You may see the Seychelles magpie robin on the coastal plateau, one of the rarest birds in the world. Three other unique Seychelles birdlife – a sunbird, a blue pigeon and a fody – are also found in this area. Aride's unique plants – Wright's gardenia and the newly discovered, night-flowering Aride cucumber – may also be seen. Some agriculture is also carried out in this area.

Progressing towards the western end of the plateau, you will see

Wright's gardenia

ground nesting white-tailed tropicbirds and fairy terns which precariously balance a single egg on a bare tree branch while waiting for it to hatch. Both species breed all year round.

At the western end of the plateau, the path rises fairly steeply through pisonia trees, the sticky seeds of which will sometimes ensnare careless birds. Keep to the path to avoid the burrows of Audubon's and wedge-tailed shearwaters.

The climb to the **viewing point** over Aride's northern cliffs can be tiring, especially when it is still and humid, but the view from the summit makes it all worthwhile. Here, you will see hundreds of giant primitive frigatebirds. Two species, great and lesser, roost here, though the nearest breeding site is Aldabra, 1,200km (750 miles) away. With a bit of luck you may also see hawksbill turtles in the turquoise waters below, or catch a glimpse of a red-tailed tropicbird, which has its only breeding site in the region on Aride.

You are taken back to the visitors' shelter by the same route, in time for a simple barbecue lunch provided by your boat crew. You may swim or snorkel from the beach, though you should take care

sea is rough that you do not get swept onto the bare
crops. It is also unsafe to swim near the edges of the island
he currents can be strong. If in any doubt, consult the war-
ie reef off Aride is excellent, with as many as 400 species of
corded in its surrounding waters.

10. Cousin

Cousin is a nature reserve, purchased by RSNC in 1968, transferred to BirdLife International in 2003 and managed by Nature
Seychelles today. The island (28ha/69 acres) is second in impor-
tance as a seabird island only to Aride, with seven breeding
species. There are rare land birds and important nesting beaches
for hawksbill turtles. This is a half-day trip.

Roosting fairy terns

*Trips to Cousin are easily arranged through
hotels or travel agents on Praslin. Landing is
generally possible all year around. The cost
of your excursion includes a landing fee
payable to Nature Seychelles.*

On arrival, your boat will anchor close to
the island where you will transfer onto
the the island's boat and land on a sandy
beach. From here you will be guided to the
boat shed. Tours are given in English and French and you
are not allowed to wander at will. Dress in shorts or swimwear and
T-shirt and take a plastic bag to protect valuables, cameras and
film when landing and leaving, as well as sun cream and a towel.
Remember that flash photography is not permitted on the island.

Along the coastal plateau you will see many introduced plants
such as cotton, pawpaw and castor oil – remnants of the days when
the island was run as a plantation. You will also see indigenous
trees such as the tortoise tree, so-called because the smelly fruits resemble the shell of a tortoise. The fruits are also eaten by giant land
tortoises, a few of which can be seen on the island.

In this area you will also see Seychelles warblers, the species
which – due to the threat of imminent extinction – inspired a
worldwide campaign to raise the £15,000 needed to buy the island.
The campaign raised about a third of this sum, Cadbury's Choco-
lates donated another third, and Christopher Cadbury personally
gave the final sum needed to save the warbler and the island. Seychelles magpie robins also breed here, following a successful transfer project.

Other land birds in this area are the Seychelles fody – found only
here and on a few other islands – and the Madagascar turtle dove.
Breeding sea birds include the lesser noddy during the southeast
monsoon and fairy tern all year round. Other creatures include numerous lizards, giant millipedes and especially the Seychelles skink
and Wright's skink.

Hawksbill turtle

A short, easy walk uphill leads to the summit of the island at 69m (225ft) above sea level. This affords views towards neighbouring **Cousine** island.

Return to the beach; if you are lucky you may encounter a hawksbill turtle, mainly during the months of October–March. Do not approach a turtle coming up the beach in case you scare it back into the sea. Once the turtle has started to lay, it becomes almost oblivious to your presence.

11. Curieuse and St Pierre

Visit Curieuse, a former leper colony and home to many giant land tortoises. Take a board walk through the mangrove swamp; then visit the coral reefs of St Pierre to see one of the best snorkelling spots in the granite islands.

If you also decide to visit Cousin as a morning trip, you can proceed from there to Curieuse and St Pierre for the afternoon. These three combined make an excellent full-day trip. If you decide to do just this trip as a half day on its own, we recommend that you hire a small boat for the morning to avoid the much busier afternoons when other boats arrive. Many small boats are available to take you across to Curieuse. Ask at your hotel reception or one of the tour agents for details.

A trip to Cousin, Curieuse and St Pierre will usually include a Creole barbecue at Curieuse. The food is good but fairly basic with soft drinks provided.

You will land on **Curieuse** at **Anse St José**, facing Praslin. Look for the renovated plantation house, known as the **Doctor's House** and now turned into an information centre, which dominates the shady barbecue site. A short walk away at the western end of the beach are ruins of houses that once belonged to a former leper colony.

The best walk heads inland from the right-hand side of the Doctor's House. There is another ruined building on the right, just before the path climbs upwards. Follow the path up, then down towards a **board walk** through mangroves. Take care on the boards as some are loose; it is best to stick to the centre. Bear right at the walk's T-junction and

Board walk through mangroves

Barbecue on Curieuse

walk along the wall which crosses **Laraie Bay**. This is an old turtle pond – now abandoned – where turtles were kept alive prior to shipment. Today, turtles may occasionally be seen swimming freely inside the pond, having entered during the high tide. It is also possible to see many colourful reef fish, including parrot fish, moray eels and Moorish idols. Indeed, this is one of the few places in Seychelles where you can go fish watching without getting wet.

From here you can see the hills of Curieuse, which are heavily degraded compared to other Seychelles islands. However, coco de mer palms may be seen, this being the only island other than Praslin where they occur naturally.

Reaching the opposite side, the path winds its way through some strange but natural rock sculptures. Look out for an area where there is a wedge of coral about 3m (10ft) above the high tide mark. Samples from sites such as this have been dated as being about 6,000 years old.

Curiously, sea levels in Seychelles have fallen since then, whereas worldwide they have been rising. In Seychelles, the ocean level is 5m (16ft) lower than it is off India while sea levels at Praslin and Curieuse are 1m (3ft) lower than at Mahé. The best possible explanation for this is a change in ocean currents.

Tortoise project signboard

A short distance further on, at **Grand Anse**, you reach the **giant land tortoise research centre**. Here, in pens, you can see tortoises from one to five years old. Many, a lot older and larger are roaming loose, brought here from Aldabra. There are also displays of coco de mer nuts, though these are not on sale. Return to Anse St José by the same route.

After this invigorating walk, now it is time for a refreshing swim. Rejoin your boat to get to **St Pierre**. The corals here have suffered some damage from souvenir hunters but the numbers and variety of fish is amazing and this remains one of the best snorkelling sites in the granite islands. Be content just to look and not touch. You will return to Praslin at about 5pm.

Slumbering giant land tortoises

CORAL ISLANDS

12. Bird Island

To get a complete picture of Seychelles, you must visit at least one coral island. If time is limited, you should make it this one. A colony of a million sooty terns is present from April–October (the best time to visit). The beaches are pristine and there is excellent swimming and snorkelling, or fishing if you wish. Visitors are always refreshed by the feeling of having escaped from the rat race – it seems that the rest of the world simply disappears.

A minimum stay of one night at Bird Island Lodge, the only accommodation on the island, is necessary as there is only one flight per day departing Mahé at 10.30am and returning from Bird at 11.15am. Flying time is 30 minutes. Bookings for flights and accommodation can be made through a travel agent, the Bird Island Lodge at tel: 323322, e-mail: birdland@seychelles.net, www.BirdIslandSeychelles.com or Wildlife Tours, Kingsgate House, Victoria at tel: 224925.

Bird is a flat, coralline island 98km (60 miles) northwest of Mahé. In size it is just 1½km (1 mile) by ½km (¼ mile), taking its name from the island's enormous sooty tern colony. For bird-watchers, October is the best month, combining the spectacle of the tern colony with the chance of seeing rare migrants. Non-birders can simply enjoy the feeling of remoteness and the wild beauty of the island.

On arrival, you are met by the manager of the lodge and escorted to your chalet. After settling in, assuming you are on Bird at the same time as the sooty terns, you will probably be drawn to investigate the colony by the noise emanating from it. Walk to the restaurant and up the beach, away from the hotel buildings. After about 200m (220yds), a sign points inland to a **viewing platform** from where you can watch the action. Even if you miss the sign, the thousands of birds plying back and forth between the colony and the sea will lead you to the spot.

Sooty tern eggs are considered a great delicacy by the Seychellois, which meant that

Sooty terns

Esmeralda, the world's largest tortoise

the Bird Island colony was once heavily exploited. Fortunately, today, the precious eggs are protected by the island's owners. A small number of eggs are taken from areas peripheral to the main colony for use at the lodge; and tern eggs sometimes feature on the menu there.

Return to the lodge and ask at the reception desk about the last reported whereabouts of the island's most famous resident, **Esmeralda**, one of the three well-known giant land tortoises which roam around Bird. Esmeralda (who is a male, despite the name), tips the scales at a hefty 304kg (670lbs), once making him officially the world's heaviest tortoise. Another reptile, the hawksbill turtle, commonly hauls itself up the beach to lay eggs between October and April. The sight of this endangered creature may be some compensation for missing the tern colony, if you cannot time your visit for that.

All meals, simply prepared using fresh ingredients grown on the island like pawpaw, okra, pumpkin, aubergine and chillies, are included in your stay. There is also a small pig and poultry farm, and fish is never a problem; a fresh supply arrives at the lodge's doorstep every day.

If you stay for a few days, you could enjoy a fishing trip. Just north of Bird, the **Seychelles Bank** slips away to a tremendous depth. A 4-hour trip will take

A fiery Bird Island sunset

you to fishing grounds where sailfish, dorado, bonito and other game fish are plentiful. Depending on the time of the year, whales and dolphins can also be sometimes seen.

There is some good snorkelling, and equipment is available from the reception desk. Ask here for details of the best spots, as conditions change throughout the year and there are sometimes strong currents in certain areas.

Keen bird-watchers should walk to the northern end of the island and check the bushes and scan the sandbanks for waders, and the airstrip – when there are no flights – for passerines. However, the usual thing on Bird is for people to do very little indeed; read a book, swim, wander along the beach looking for shells, watch the sunset, and fall asleep at night listening to the lapping of waves.

13. Desroches

Desroches is the exposed rim of a submerged atoll in the Amirantes Group, lying 230km (144 miles) southwest of the granitic islands. The Desroches Island Resort is situated at one extremity of the island which is 6km (3½ miles) long and 1km (½ mile) wide. There are stunning beaches, superb diving and other watersports. A minimum stay of 2 days is necessary.

There are four flights a week; on Monday, Wednesday, Friday and Sunday from Mahé. Bookings for flights and accommodation can be made through the Desroches Island Resort at tel: 229003, e-mail: desroches@seychelles.net. All flights depart at 1pm and return by 3pm the same day. Flying time is about 45 minutes.

Rustic Desroches Lodge's chalets

You will be met by the Desroches Lodge's manager on arrival and escorted to the reception for a welcome drink and check-in. Your booking includes all meals. Lunch is a buffet and dinner may be a candle-lit barbecue – weather permitting – or taken in the restaurant. Naturally, evening entertainment is limited.

Diving is best during October–April when you can explore the **Drop**, an atoll wall. From May to September, diving within the shallow lagoon is possible. The lodge's dive centre is well-equipped, and for non-divers, there are Hobiecats, canoes and water scooters for hire, or you can go paragliding, water skiing or deep-sea fishing. Records have been set in Desroches' relatively unfished waters and plaques on the watersports centre testify to this.

The easiest way to explore the island is on a bicycle, which you can borrow from the reception desk. Avoid riding out during the hottest part of the day. Also, be warned that the tracks are bumpy and some peter out completely or are blocked by logs. They can also be muddy after heavy rain, so take care. To reach the **Settle-**

ment, you can either cycle or walk – it is within easy walking distance, all on flat land – to the **airstrip** and take the track that is located near the centre of the island and which runs parallel to the coast, through coconut plantation.

Seychelles lily

Relax on Desroches stunning talcum powder beaches

The Settlement is the area where plantation workers have their houses, with a few facilities such as a lock-up, 'hospital' (no equipment, just two rooms with beds), a shop which opens once a week (selling rice, sugar and a few basics) and farm buildings such as the copra drier.

En route to the Settlement, you pass through a forest of coconut palms. Coconuts used to be the mainstay of the island's economy and some copra is still produced. The *kalorifer* at the Settlement is still used though the oil press inland of this, on the opposite side of the path from the coast, is now overgrown. About 40 people work at the Settlement, growing vegetables and tending livestock to supply the lodge; the surplus is exported to Mahé.

There is little to see beyond the Settlement, apart from an automatic **Lighthouse** at the far end of the island. There is a ladder to the top if you want to get a good view of both sides of the island at once. Just follow the beach or the coastal track down the island to reach it.

Swimming and snorkelling is safe all the way along the inner edge of the lagoon; usually the waters here are as still as a mill pond, especially during the southeast monsoon from April–September, when the prevailing wind is from the opposite side of the island.

Desroches has the same sort of Robinson Crusoe atmosphere as Bird's. The difference is that Desroches is a former plantation and you get to see the remains of a past way of life here. Still, even in this isolated haven, there is a sense that Desroches is a shadow of its former self.

A lone trumpetfish

58

14. Alphonse

This is the ultimate 'get away from it' all island, lying 400km (250 miles) southwest of Mahé. Shaped like an arrow head, with skeins of white sand trailing away from the leading tip, Alphonse is the largest island of the group, which also bears its name. The group also includes the islands of Bijoutier and St Francois. The beaches are splendid, the diving spectacular, while watersports include the best fly fishing in the Indian Ocean.

Days and times of flights should be checked with agents 7° South Ltd at tel: 322682. Flying time is approximately one hour. Accommodation is available at Alphonse Island Resort and reservations may be made through 7° South Ltd or direct with Alphonse Island Resort Ltd at tel: 323220, e-mail: alphonse@seychelles.net.

Upon arrival on **Alphonse**, you are met by staff from **Alphonse Island Resort** and escorted to reception for a welcome drink and check in. All bookings are full board.

Diving may be arranged through the watersports centre. Currents can be strong and times of dives may vary according to tides. The atoll wall is resplendent with a forest of Gorgonian fan corals inhabited by colourful reef life. Nearby, large shoals of fish may be seen, including barracuda. Altogether, diving here is far more thrilling than in the granitic islands. For the less experienced, diving and snorkelling is also possible within the safety of the lagoon.

Colourful angelfish

Watersports also include big game fishing and the best fly fishing imaginable at neighbouring **St Francois**. The atoll between St Francois and **Bijoutier** is a natural reservoir, where bone fish weighing up to 6kg (15lbs) and trevally more than 35kg (77lbs) can be found. Some beginners have caught as many as 20 bone fish on their first day, while more experienced fishermen may easily net 50 or more. Numbers are limited to 12 people on the flats at any one time, and all catches are released. A motor yacht departs daily at about 7am. Passengers then transfer to flat boats which may be run into very shallow water almost anywhere in the lagoon. The return trip to Alphonse is about 4.30pm.

Apart from the fly fishing, St Francois is spectacular for the number of shipwrecks submerged in its reef. Just a short distance offshore is one of the deepest areas of the Indian Ocean, the **Amirantes Trench**, more than 5km (3 miles) deep. Many a sailor has been caught unawares by this sudden transition from exposed reef to tremendous depths. The horizon may be forbidding, with its rim of boiling white waters, but ashore on the island all that disturbs the peace is the chirping of sparrows. In our opinion, this is the most beautiful island in Seychelles, never inhabited save for shipwrecked mariners awaiting rescue. For many, Bijoutier would take this title because of its classic tropic-isle shape, topped with emerald green palms and fringed with a circlet of white sand. Excursions can be arranged to Bijoutier and St Francois, but the latter is difficult to reach except at spring tides.

Back on Alphonse, land lubbers may explore the **Old Settlement** adjacent to the airstrip. There is an old *kalorifer* where copra, once the mainstay of the outer islands, was produced. Several paths lead off into the undergrowth. Near the **Chemin Madam** are the poignant remains of the **island cemetery**, a stark reminder of how hard life was when the island was inhabited in the past. Volcy Frichot was only three months old when he died in 1908. Henry Joseph's is one of the oldest graves. He was born in Africa, and it is possible he was one of those liberated by the British from Arab slavers in the 1860s, and brought to Alphonse as a labourer.

The waters of the lagoon are warm and shallow, and the swimming is safe, (though there are many baby reef sharks). Sometimes there is a lot of seaweed on the beach, washed up by offshore currents. The spacious, air-conditioned bungalows of the resort mean visitors can enjoy these islands in comfort. A walk up the concrete airstrip is a useful shortcut from one side of the island to the other (bearing in mind its practical purpose, though there is no more than one flight per day). The little birds flitting through the grass on either side of the airstrip are waxbills, not found on any of the other outer islands. The airstrip itself is frequented by migratory birds and several rarities have been reported on Alphonse.

Alphonse – the ultimate getaway

15. Nature Walks

To reach some of Seychelles' wildest and most atmospheric places, you need to walk. You will see plants and animals found nowhere else on earth and experience the quiet beauty of the forest.

The Tourism Division has a series of excellent illustrated booklets on Seychelles' flora and fauna on sale at their shop in Independence House, Victoria, Mahé. Alternatively, contact Basil Beaudouin (tel: 241790), a knowlegeable guide who knows all the trails well, and can identify most of the 250 indigenous species of plants you may see. Beaudouin leads walks of varying difficulty, lasting from as little as 1–2 hours to as long as 6–8 hours.

Glacis viewed on the Anse Major walk

The best season for walking is during the cooler, less humid months from June–September. The worst time is at the height of the rains, from mid-December–January, when paths are muddy and slippery. April is also a difficult month because humidity is high and there is precious little breeze to cool you. Avoid the middle of the day for your trek; early morning and late afternoon is best. Remember, it gets dark under the trees by about 6.30pm.

You will need a good pair of shoes for most walks, except for the Danzil-Anse Major walk where ordinary flip flops will do. Walking boots are probably a bit over the top but a decent pair of trainers with a good grip are fine. You will need a hat, sunglasses, a bottle of water and a snack to enjoy when you reach the top, or the end.

Do not overestimate your fitness: most walks are steep, the paths very uneven and the climate very different for strenuous activity than most of Europe and the US. The humidity, in particular, is taxing. In the mountains, look carefully when looking for hand-holds. The endemic palms have spines and tree branches are often rotten and may break off in your hand. Do not attempt any walk – except the Danzil-Anse Major path – after rain as the paths will be dangerous.

Danzil-Anse Major Walk: An easy walk along almost the only stretch of Mahé's coast with no road access. It leads to a small secluded beach. There is little shade, so leave early or wait until about 3pm. Keep an eye on your valuables at Anse Major. It would be better for women not to do the walk alone in case you get hassled.

The walk starts at **Auberge Club des Seychelles**, at the end of the road from Beau Vallon to Bel Ombre. You can park where the road widens at the end, just by **Scala Restaurant**, and walk up the hill past the hotel. If you are travelling by bus, the bus stop is just here also. Ask for Scala Restaurant.

Follow the road up the hill; soon it becomes a track and then a well marked path, crossing the Danzil River. Highlights of the walk include wonderful views of Beau Vallon and Silhouette island, and spectacular areas of granitic rock slopes known as *glacis*. It should take about 1½ hours to reach Anse Major at a leisurely pace. You return by the same route. There are no facilities at Anse Major, so you may wish to take along food and drink.

La Reserve and Brulee Walk: This is Mahé's answer to Praslin's Vallée de Mai; the island's best area of palm forest, with five of Seychelles' six unique palm species – only the coco de mer is missing. There are view-points over vertical granite cliffs which are sometimes adorned with shy sprays of flowering orchids.

The starting point is reached from Victoria by driving south and taking the **Montagne Posee Road** at Anse aux Pins, just after the old plantation house with the sign 'Lenstiti Kreol'. Close to the summit of this pass is a signboard on the left for Cable and Wireless. Park on the left, just inside the entrance. Do not block the access. The trail begins here, climbing the steep hill to the left under mahogany trees.

It is quite well signposted, but without the detailed booklet (or the help of a guide) there are two points where you may go wrong. First, after you have climbed the short, steep hill, you will come out onto a rocky area. Turn 90 degrees to the left and you will pick up the trail running along the edge of the mahogany plantation (even if you are not a botanist, you can recognise the plantation by the ordered ranks of the trees, in comparison with the general untidiness of wild woodland). The second danger spot is about 150m (164yds) further on, where the trail turns 90 degrees to the right. There is supposed to be a post here with an arrow pointing uphill but it is not obvious if you are not looking for it, and occasionally it falls down.

From here, the trail is well marked and obvious. The next 150m (164yds) are the most difficult, being quite steep and a bit slippery. Then the path levels out through a beautiful area of palm forest for about another 200m (220yds) before turning uphill again. On this stretch you have a choice. A sign points to the

Footpath and sign for La Reserve

left, indicating a circular path marked with green spots. We suggest that if you are flagging at this point, you keep straight on, following the yellow spots up the there-and-back path to the viewing point. This overlooks Anse Boileau and the islands of Ile aux Vaches, Thérese and Conception.

To the right of Conception is Morne Blanc, then **Morne Seychellois**, the highest point for 1,000 miles around. This walk should take about 1½ hours up and an hour down.

Tea Factory-Morne Blanc Walk: This is a short, sharp climb to the summit of a mountain, which from the west coast looks unassailable. However, the track behind this vertical face is not too dif-

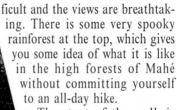

ficult and the views are breathtaking. There is some very spooky rainforest at the top, which gives you some idea of what it is like in the high forests of Mahé without committing yourself to an all-day hike.

The start of the walk is close to the **Seychelles Tea and Coffee Company** on the **Sans Souci** Road. From here, it is about 200m (220yds) in the direction of Victoria.

Mighty Morne Blanc

The path rises to 250m (820ft) from the road to a height of 667m (2,188ft) above sea level. The walk is within **Morne Seychellois National Park** and you will see many of Seychelles' unique plants and hear frogs croaking but see surprisingly few birds. You may also see Seychelles wolf snakes and possibly the Seychelles house snake (though this is less likely as they are nocturnal); both are harmless.

From the summit you can see both sides of Mahé at once. The islands of St Anne Marine National Park are to the east and most of the west coast as far as Ansé la Mouche will be in view. Silhouette island is also visible to the right. Take care at the summit. The cliff you are standing on is almost vertical and it is a long way down. Return via the same route. It should take about an hour to reach the top and about half that to descend; and much less if you are careless on the cliff top!

The best mist forest can be discovered only with a guide, on **Congo Rouge**, a grade 3 walk, taking 3 to 6 hours. This particular walk should never be attempted without a guide, as it is easy to get lost, unlike the usual tourist trails.

Visiting a mist forest is a unique experience and a total contrast with the atmosphere of the beach. The trees are covered in moss, from which water can be squeezed like a wet sponge. It is almost always totally silent, apart from the high-pitched piping of the frogs. Chamelons, leaf insects, stick insects and pitcher plants inhabit this almost ethereal mountain world.

16. Diving

Seychelles is probably one of the best places in the world to learn how to dive. The water is warm and usually clear, the underwater scenery superb and the facilities excellent. Much of the best diving is to be had on shallow reefs, ideal for beginners.

We recommend the **Seychelles Underwater Centre** (tel: 247357, daily 8.30am–5pm) at Coral Strand Hotel, Beau Vallon, Mahé, because we both learned to dive here. Having subsequently dived in many places the world over, we have yet to find its equal for standards of safety, equipment and friendliness.

If you are not sure, take the 1-day introductory course available on weekdays. You start at 9am with a pool dive in the swimming pool to familiarise yourself with the equipment and learn the basics of scuba techniques. After a break for lunch, you are off on a boat dive into a shallow reef with your instructor, returning to shore at about 3.30pm. There is no certificate issued at this level, but it does let you know what diving is all about: you can dive again but always supervised by an instructor.

If you decide to take the plunge, you will spend 4 days obtaining a PADI Open Water Certificate which will enable you to dive worldwide. These courses are available on request and run every week. There are five theory sessions, five pool sessions and four open sea dives. The price of the course includes a diving manual, full equipment rental and all dives. Courses are run in English, French and German. Other more advanced PADI courses are also available.

Having learned to dive, you can really explore the wonders of the coral reef. The reefs around the granite islands are pretty rather than spectacular, in comparison with the Red Sea for example, but the numbers and variety of fish species is tremendous. Seychelles Underwater Centre runs trips to 30 inshore sites (6–25m depth) and 12 offshore sites (15–30m depth) for certified divers. Live aboard charters to more remote destinations can be arranged by the centre.

17. Watersports

The same good reasons apply for enjoying watersports in Seychelles as for diving. The weather is good, the sea is warm and inviting and the facilities are excellent.

The best equipment and widest range of activities are offered on **Beau Vallon** beach on **Mahé**, but most large hotels and island lodges carry some decent equipment.

Leisure 2000 (tel: 247046) of Beau

Paraglider at Beau Vallon

Vallon are the only APA (American Paragliding Association) internationally qualified paragliding operation in Seychelles. Situated next to Coral Strand Hotel, they have discounted rates for hotel residents and those staying at Auberge Club des Seychelles, Fisherman's Cove, Sunset Beach and Vista Bay Club.

There are no motorised watersports available before noon on weekdays, so as not to interfere with the nets of the mackerel fishermen. Apart from this restriction, Leisure 2000 is open daily (10am–5pm) except 1 January. Motorised sports on offer after the restricted hours are water skiing and water scooters. Hobiecats, windsurfers, canoes and bellyboards can be hired by the hour and snorkelling equipment by the day. For novices, Hobiecat, windsurfing and skiing lessons are available from Leisure 2000.

Beau Vallon is not always the best place to play in the sea. It is quite sheltered during May–October. There is no point hiring a windsurfer if the sea is like a mill pond. By the same token, you may think twice about paragliding in unsettled weather.

18. Deep Sea Fishing

Seychelles offers excellent opportunities for big game fishing. Possible catches include sailfish, kingfish, shark, dorado, bonito, and occasionally marlin, depending on the season.

You can fish all year round, although unsettled weather during the peak of the rainy season (mid-December to end of January) can cause cancellations on occasion. If you are

Fishing around

staying in the Beau Vallon area, we recommend using the services of **Jimmy Mancienne** (mobile tel: 510269), whose shop is next to the **Boat House** restaurant north of the Coral Strand Hotel where the coast road turns inland towards Victoria. It is best to call at the shop (open daily 8.30am–6pm) and discuss your plans. Special programmes can be arranged to suit you personally and can include trips to other islands and snorkelling. Departure and return times are flexible.

Mancienne operates the boat *Bluefin*, a 15-m (47-ft) catamaran which carries up to 20 passengers and permits eight fishing rods to be used at any one time.

Fishing trips can be arranged any day, subject to availability. Lunch and soft drinks are included in the price together with island landing fees, if applicable. Trips usually depart at 8am and return in the evening at 5pm. Fishing is best up to noon and then from 3pm onwards, so an island visit for lunch makes a good break at a time when there is little action. August–December is best for sailfish, January–March for kingfish (or wahoo), November–December for *karang* (or trevally). Other fish like tuna, bonito and dorado may be caught all year around.

Night fishing trips – the price includes snacks and soft drinks – may also be arranged, departing at 5pm and returning around midnight. You can go bottom fishing for red snapper, known locally as

bourzwa, and green jobfish or *zob*. You can choose to bring your catch on board or cast it back to fight another day. On return to Beau Vallon, you may keep all or some of your catch as you wish. No fish will be wasted, you can be sure.

No previous experience is necessary and the friendly, helpful boatmen are happy to give instruction for no extra charge. The boats carry all the necessary safety equipment, first-aid kits and a radio link. If you arrange to have snorkelling included in your trip, this equipment can also be included if you inform them beforehand.

On Mahé, other game fishing boats include *Striker2*, a high-speed 9-m (30-ft) catamaran based at Coral Strand Hotel, operated by **Leslie Pool** (tel: 247848 or

Caught unawares

mobile: 511958), who offers half-day or full-day trips; the latter includes a barbecue lunch on Silhouette island. **Island Charters (Seychelles) Ltd** (tel: 280000 or mobile: 515278) operates a luxurious, well-equipped 13-m (40-ft) high-speed sports fishing catamaran.

On Praslin, we recommend **William Rose** (tel: 232329) who runs a variety of trips. Fishing on Denis, Bird, Alphonse and Desroches islands is excellent and each resort can arrange trips for guests.

19. Cruising

If you have the time and money, this can be the experience of a lifetime. You will see some of the world's most remote and beautiful islands, many of which are uninhabited. Cruising arrangements should be made well in advance. There are several liveaboard charter boats – which include diving – based in Seychelles. Bookings can be made through local travel agents or directly with the boat owners.

There are a number of varied options. For excursions around the granitic islands, the most beautiful boats are operated by **Silhouette Cruises Ltd** (tel: 324026 or mobile: 514051). These are the twin-masted schooners *Sea Shell* and *Sea Pearl*. Charters are usually 5 or 6 days, and the itinerary varies according to the season. If you wish to see a number of the islands, then this can be the best way to achieve it within a short period, thereby avoiding the hassle of having to transfer between hotels. The boats are also fully equipped for diving and watersports activities.

Water World (Pty) Ltd (tel: 373766) runs several vessels, notably the 16-m (50-ft) luxury motor yacht *Shamal*, which cruises at 24 knots. With just three double cabins for passengers, this is an exclusive if somewhat expensive way to cruise, but minimum time is wasted in transit.

VPM (tel: 225676) and **Sunsail** (tel: 225700) operate fleets of catamarans and monohulls available either for bare boat charter or with a qualified skipper.

Aldabra, the world's largest raised atoll, is the Holy Grail for the cruising fraternity. Attractions here include superb diving, the world's largest population of giant tortoises (about 100,000, several times more than the Galapagos) and the last surviving flightless bird of the Indian Ocean region, the Aldabra Rail.

Indian Ocean Explorer (tel: 345445) runs trips to Aldabra, Cosmoledo and Astove. This is a specialist dive boat, but also offers customised itineraries for private charters. No other vessel offers scheduled trips to this remote corner of Seychelles, though **High Aspect** (mobile tel: 513911), a luxury sailing yacht for up to eight guests, offers customised trips to as far afield as Kenya.

The best time for cruising is mid-September to mid-December. Thereafter until March, there can be unsettled weather and a risk of cyclones in the southern islands. April–May is also another good period to go out to sea. However, from June to mid-September, the southeast monsoon brings rough seas which are uncomfortable for long passages. It is therefore essential to book well in advance for live-aboard charters. Shorter excursions can usually be arranged with less notice.

Cruise yacht leaving Victoria

Shopping

There is very little in the way of traditional handicrafts or gifts that are special to Seychelles. The souvenir industry is a fairly recent phenomenon which has sprung up in response to the growth in tourism. It is worth having a good look around and visiting many of the artisans themselves before deciding what to buy. Prices are usually fixed and generally high, though some street traders may load their prices in response to tourist expectations that they should bargain. In shops, you should not expect any bargaining. The products listed below are found almost exclusively on Mahé, with the exception of the coco de mer nuts. Shopping in Praslin is expensive and the range of items is small. Shopping is very limited on the other islands.

A splash of local colour

What to Buy

Batiks

Ron Gerlach uses this Indonesian technique to produce a product that is uniquely Seychellois. His studio (Monday–Friday 10am–12.30pm, 1.30–5pm, Saturday 10am–12.30pm, closed Sunday), is on Beau Vallon beach, halfway between the Coral Strand Hotel and the Baobab Pizzeria. Gerlach is Chairman of the Nature Protection Trust of Seychelles.

Ron Gerlach sun-drying batik.

Stained Glass

Les and Sharon Masterson produce stained glass mobiles, panels, suncatchers, windows and lightshades featuring local birds and fish at their studio **Thoughts** (tel: 224060, daily 9am–9pm), on the Sans Souci Road. These are also available from shops including **Wild Ginger** at Beau Vallon (tel: 247332, daily 10.30am– 8pm; Sunday 10.30am–6pm).

From top: Nourrice with his work, pottery and woven crafts at codevar, fiery spices, evocative perfumes and model boats

Art

Several artists are mentioned in the Mahé *Itinerary 1*. These include **Colbert Nourrice**, whose highly original paintings tell stories of events from his life. The work of **Egbert Marday**, can be seen at his home studio, **Kreation Beau-et-Mien**, Helvetia, La Misere (tel: 378456 or mobile: 512792), where he has both paintings and sculptures. Other artists' work can be viewed at **Wild Ginger** (in Beau Vallon), including Barbara Jenson, Andre Gee, Roxy Athanase and Colbert Nourrice.

Pottery

Wild Ginger at Beau Vallon, **Later Rouz** at the Craft Village and **Codevar** at Camion Hall, Victoria, sell attractive and unusual pottery items. These are made by **Seypot** at Union Vale, Mahé.

Woven Crafts and Mats

Woven table mats, hats and baskets are inexpensive. **Codevar** and other shops have a good selection. The kiosks of **Fiennes Esplanade**, Victoria, have hats and other woven items.

Mats printed with beautiful photographs of Seychelles may be purchased from **Photo Eden**, Independence Avenue, Victoria. Photo Eden also carries a variety of other gifts, such as large photograph albums with a map of Mahé embossed on the covers.

Some people like to take home the local grass brushes, the *zig* and the *fatak*. Locally made ones are usually on sale on the edges of the market on Saturday mornings.

Tea and Spices

Seychelles Tea and Coffee Company sell packs of teas with vanilla, lemon, orange and cinnamon flavours. A packet with all the ingredients you need to make a real Seychelles curry, including cinnamon bark, the *kari pile* and other spices, can be bought at **Victoria market** (especially the stalls to the right of the Market Street entrance). Here, you can also buy a coconut stool, with a sharp spike attached at one end for grating coconuts. There are also dried vanilla pods for sale.

69

The appropriately named 'Hellfire' on sale at the market is pickled hot chillies. This is something that we find ourselves constantly taking home for friends who miss their 'real' chilli sauce dearly.

Perfumes

Kreol Fleurage Parfums of North East Point, Mahé (tel: 241329), produces three perfumes using no fewer than 102 local plants, 35 percent of which have never previously been used for perfumes. The perfumes are also on sale in many hotel and souvenir shops.

Model Boats

La Marine, mentioned in Mahe *Itinerary 1*, produces excellent but very expensive model boats based on actual historical vessels.

Jewellery

Kreolor (tel: 344551) have shops at Camion Hall, Victoria and at La Passe on La Digue. Kreolor items are also on sale at **Galerie des Artes** on Praslin. Kreolor manufactures beautiful jewellery, combining gold with mother of pearl, sea shells and other local items. It also manufactures some highly original items, combining granite, raffia seeds, coconut wood and espadon. Espadon is the bill of sailfish discarded by fishermen, which looks like ivory and makes an attractive and unusual souvenir special to Seychelles.

Praslin Ocean Farm Ltd (tel: 233150) culture pearls from the local black-tipped pearl oyster. It produces silvery blue, green, gold and black coloured pearls which are set in exquisite jewellery and also baby clams plated with silver and gold. Their shop, **Black Pearls of Seychelles** is opposite the Praslin airstrip and is worth visiting not only to see the jewellery, but also their aquarium.

Coco de Mer

The best place to buy a whole coco de mer is the **Forestry Station**, Fond B'Offay, Praslin (Monday–Friday 8am–4pm). They are also available in almost every tourist shop, polished and unpolished. You must make sure that the vendor gives you an export certificate to go with the nut, or you will have problems with customs. Remember that the little ones are not genuine; they are made out of wood. Some nuts have been hollowed out so that they are lighter for carriage, and unless you want a door stop, it is probably best to buy one of these. You will also see items such as fruit bowls or vases made out of coco de mer.

Going nutty

Clothing

If you look carefully, you will find items which are genuinely locally produced, ie, the fabric is printed and sewn in Seychelles.

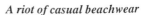

A riot of casual beachwear

Sunstroke Boutique in Market Street carries a wide range of T-shirts, beachwear, shorts, dresses etc, many of which are very original. **Carina** at the Craft Village does a range of hand-dyed clothing in pastel colours. Numerous shops stock T-shirts and beach wear with a Seychelles theme. **Brijals**, Jivan Building, Church Street, will reproduce your holiday snap on a T-shirt.

Candles

Tropical Collection (tel: 324494) have a shop in Camion Hall, Victoria, where they sell beautiful candles in which shells have been imbedded. These shells have been taken from the sea shore, not from live animals, so you can buy them with a clear conscience.

Alcoholic Drinks

There is a delicious liqueur made from the flesh of the coconut, called Coco d'Amour, in a coco de mer shaped bottle, which is widely available in the shops. There are a whole range of exciting liqueurs made by **Spirit Artisanals** (tel: 324556), Union Vale, which are also on sale at Beau Vallon's **Wild Ginger** and many other outlets. Flavours include passion fruit, guava, mango, mint, chocolate, lemon, ginger and cinnamon.

Miscellaneous Souvenirs

The larger souvenir shops such as **Wild Ginger** (Beau Vallon), **Codevar** (at Camion Hall) and the various outlets in the **Craft Village** sell a range of novel products, including soaps scented with local perfumes and essential oils, wooden fish, towels, keyrings, hand-painted glasses, mirrors, jewellery, stamps, first day covers, batik goods, bags and dolls. There are many smaller shops dotted around the islands which will carry similar goods.

What Not To Buy

Corals, coral jewellery and shells look very attractive at the stalls but once again, what you are looking at are rows of dead bodies. Local reefs remain attractive and relatively unexploited because tourism is quite a new phenomenon here, but if the demand for coral and shells is sustained or begins to grow, the reefs here will be decimated as they have been in so many other places. If you are still pondering, remember that Seychelles is a middle-income country and it does not need to sacrifice its natural assets and beauty to ensure the daily survival of its people.

Eating Out

The Seychellois are among the world's greatest per capita consumers of fish. The reason for this one-food obsession is its availability and quality. The fish in Seychelles is really more flavourful than those found in other waters. Amongst the best tasting fish is red snapper (*bourzwa*) – although the French spelling, *bourgeois*, is often used on menus. The white-fleshed job – Creole *zob* – is also very tasty. Steaks from larger fish are also nearly always available, in particular tuna. Those who have never had a tuna steak are often surprised by just how meaty it is in taste and texture. Other excellent fish steaks come from kingfish – the local name for what Americans call wahoo, and *karang* – known elsewhere as trevally – and usually on the menu under the French spelling, *carangue*.

Local fish is excellent

Surprisingly, apart from fish, there is not a great deal of local seafood around for a mid-ocean country. Lobster is almost always imported as local stocks have been over-fished. Crabs are in fairly plentiful supply and local prawns are usually available in restaurants from a prawn farm on Coetivy island.

There are just two species of shellfish used regularly in cooking. One is the *tektek*, a small burrowing shellfish found on sandy beaches and the other, which looks like a small clam, is the *palourd*. *Tektek* is always served in soup, stewed with onions, garlic, ginger and parsley. *Palourd*, most often served soaking in aromatic garlic butter, is a great starter.

Octopus in Seychelles is superb. If you have tried it elsewhere and dismissed it as chewy and rubbery, give it another chance in Seychelles. It makes a delicious starter in octopus salad or as a main course in a curry cooked with coconut milk. Either way, it will melt in your mouth.

If you are trying out the local cui-

A Seychellois housewife cooking up a storm

A no-holds-barred champagne brunch

sine, there should be a little dish of chilli sauce somewhere on the table. Take it easy until you've sampled a little, even if you like hot food. The tiny Seychelles chillies are like dynamite. Likewise, local curries are quite hot, but we find them delicious and full of flavour.

Starters will often include *palmis*, or millionaire's salad, the living shoot of the coconut palm cut into wafer thin strips. Raw fish marinated in lime juice is also popular.

Nearly all restaurants offer at least some meat or chicken dishes too. Make the most of the main courses and starters, because unless you are thrilled to bits by fresh tropical fruits – mango, papaya, banana, passionfruit, guava and so on – Seychelles deserts are often disappointing. The choice is usually ice cream or fruit salad.

Drinks

After dinner, you could try *citronelle* tea instead of normal tea or coffee. This is made by pouring boiling water onto lemon grass, a common but wonderfully fragrant grass found in the mountains. This refreshing infusion is also supposed to help digestion.

The locally brewed lager beers, Seybrew and Eku, are excellent as Celebration Brew, a red beer. There is a range of fizzy soft drinks available from Seybrew and other manufacturers, including Coca-Cola, Diet Coke, Sprite, Fanta, bitter lemon, fruit cocktail, ginger ale, tonic water and soda water. It is also worth asking if fresh lime or passion fruit juice is available. Freshly squeezed lime with water and a hint of sugar or salt – according to your preference – is really refreshing but very rarely on offer. Most hotels and restaurants serve fruit juices from tins or packets, although a few are now offering freshly squeezed juices. Bear in mind that wines are all imported and are very expensive when eating out.

Recommendations

The restaurants highlighted in the preceding itineraries and on the following pages represent the best of eating out in Seychelles. The

following price categories are for a three-course meal for one person, excluding drinks and service charge:
$$$ = SR300 and above;
$$ = SR200–300;
$ = SR200 and below.

A Creole buffet

Mahé

MARIE ANTOINETTE
Grand Trianon
St Louis, Mahé
Tel: 266222
Really the one restaurant you should not miss because it is the easiest place to try traditional Creole food. Marie Antoinette is situated on the hill overlooking Victoria – on the road over to Beau Vallon – and housed in a beautiful old colonial dwelling. The decor inside is simple but attractive. The menu is fixed with five small main courses, four of which are fish dishes, usually including parrot fish, tuna and *bourzwa*, and a simple dessert of fruit salad. Open every day except Sunday for lunch and dinner. It can get quite busy. *$*

Upmarket La Scala Restaurant

LA SCALA RESTAURANT
Bel Ombre, Mahé
Tel: 247535
Italian, international and sophisticated Creole cuisine. Excellent food and service. Make reservations, particularly at weekends. Open evenings only. Closed Sunday. *$$$*

The famed Marie Antoinette

THE BOAT HOUSE
Beau Vallon, Mahé
Tel: 247898
Situated on Beau Vallon beach, the evening barbecue buffet is excellent value for money. The fish is freshly caught and the side dishes make use of local produce including breadfruit, papaya and coconut. There is also plenty for both meat lovers and vegetarians. There is one sitting only at 7.30pm and it is best to book in advance. Closed Monday. *$*

LA FONTAINE
Beau Vallon, Mahé
Tel: 247841
Set back from Beau Vallon beach; serves local fish, seafood and international cuisine. Popular dishes include a seafood platter for two (consisting of lobster, octopus, smoked fish, slipper lobster and prawns), and parrot fish in banana leaf. Open daily 11am–11pm. *$$*

LE CORSAIRE RESTAURANT
Bel Ombre, Mahé
Tel: 515171
Housed in a romantic stone and thatch building, right on the ocean, this restaurant offers Italian, Creole and international cuisine. Open evenings only. Closed Monday. *$$$*

CHEZ PLUME
Anse Boileau, Mahé
Tel: 355050
The best restaurant on the west coast of Mahé. It specialises in seafood, but meat dishes are also available. Save some room, because the desserts are exceptional, particularly the passionfruit soufflé. Open evenings only. Closed Sunday. *$$*

CHEZ BATISTA
Takamaka, Mahé
Tel: 366300

Oven at Baobab Pizzeria

Very fresh fish is the speciality. Creole seafood and international cuisine in a rustic setting. *$$*

La Perle Noire
Beau Vallon, Mahé
Tel: 247046
International, Italian and sophisticated Creole cuisine. Excellent food and service. If you are fed up of fish, come here for a superb steak. If you are not fed up of fish, then they have some wonderful fish dishes too. Open daily. Evenings only. *$$$*

Baobab Pizzeria
Beau Vallon, Mahé
Tel: 247167
Good pizzas and Italian pasta dishes right on the beach – you eat with your feet in the sand. A relaxed atmosphere. Evenings only. *$*

Sam's Pizzeria
Maison Suleman,
Francis Rachel Street, Victoria
Tel: 322499
A very good restaurant with relaxed atmosphere and a varied menu. Pizzas are a speciality but there are plenty of other things to choose from. Open daily for lunch noon–2.30pm and dinner 6–10pm. *$$*

Praslin

Capri Restaurant
Grand Anse, Praslin
Tel: 233337
Situated within the Hotel Marechiaro, Capri offers an excellent range of Italian and Creole dishes in pleasant surroundings close to the beach. Open daily for lunch and dinner. *$$*

La Goulue Café
Côte D'Or, Praslin
Tel: 232223
Rustic, relaxed, outdoor setting near the beach serving mainly good quality local dishes and snacks. Open noon–9pm. Closed Sunday. *$$*

Les Rochers
La Pointe, Praslin
Tel: 233910
Located on the coast between Baie St Anne and Grand Anse, the views over what is probably the most beautiful coast on the island are superb. Serves international and Creole cuisine. Open lunch time only. Closed Sunday. *$$$*

Tante Mimi
Côte D'Or, Praslin
Tel: 232500
Certainly one of the best restaurants in Seychelles. Excellent international and Creole cuisine and fabulous décor in a magnificent, romantic colonial-style building. Pick-up and return of clients can be arranged to any Praslin hotel. Open evenings from 7.30pm, with a special Creole buffet on Wednesdays. Barbeques served on the patio Sunday lunchtime. *$$$*

Nightlife

Not surprisingly, visitors do not come to Seychelles for the nightlife. After a day of sun and sand, all but the most dedicated of party animals are too worn out for discos. Most tourists who come here have chosen Seychelles because it is unsophisticated in such respects. However, the larger hotels in Mahé and Praslin do have live bands playing a few nights a week and a few have their own discotheques.

Sometimes, there are displays of local dances, like the traditional *sega* or other activities such as limbo dancing – which seems to have nothing whatsoever to do with Seychelles at all. Smaller hotels and restaurants sometimes have a lone singer-guitarist who sings about coco de mer nuts and laments about going back to the Seychelles. It can get quite pathetic.

Night owls should not entirely despair, however. There is no need to resort to tramping up and down the beach all night with your portable CD player turned up loud. There are a few good discotheques, two casinos and a cinema in Mahé while Praslin now has two discos and a casino.

The best recommendation on islands other than Mahé or Praslin is an early night. The only nightlife provided by hotels, like a band or the odd disco, will be limited and irregular.

Locals whooping it up

Try your hand at blackjack
Nightclubs

KATIOLO CLUB
Anse Faure, Mahé
Tel: 375453
Colourful Creole-style nightclub. Friday night is Ladies' Night till 11pm. On Saturday, there may be a buffet

dinner followed by an open-air disco, weather permitting, until 3am.

FLAMBOYANT
Bois de Rose Avenue
Victoria, Mahé
Tel: 321113
The disco often features local bands on a Friday night, including some of the best musicians in Seychelles. There is ample car parking within the grounds.

JUNGLE DISCO
Grande Anse, Praslin
Mobile tel: 512683
Features a variety of dance music, both local and international. Open Friday and Saturday 10pm–4am. There are three bars and a pool room. Snacks available as well.

THE DOME NIGHTCLUB
Baie Ste Anne, Praslin
Tel: 232800
A non-smoking disco, with dazzling lighting, featuring both local and international music. There are two bars, a games room and a snack shop. Open Friday, Saturday and on the eve of public holidays. Open 10pm–4am.

Casinos

CASINO DES SEYCHELLES
Beau Vallon Bay Hotel,
Beau Vallon, Mahé
Tel: 247272
Gaming tables are open daily from 7pm–3am, slot machines from 10am. Free transport to the casino and back can be arranged from most of the hotels in Mahé. A relaxed and friendly atmosphere for amateur gamblers prevails. Dress up if you want to, but it isn't essential.

PLANTER'S CASINO
Plantation Club, PO Box 437
Baie Lazare, Mahé
Tel: 361361
Planter's is considerably more chic than Casino des Seychelles. Its gaming tables are open 8pm–2am, slot machines are open 10am–2am. Again, free transport can be arranged from Equator, Mahé Beach and Barbarons hotels.

CASINO DES ISLES
Côte D'Or, Praslin
Tel: 232500
The only casino on Praslin. As with the casinos on Mahé, the management will provide transport from and to your hotel. The excellent restaurant, Tante Mimi, is on the same premises and you could arrange to have a meal first before deciding whether you are in the mood for a flutter. Open daily 7.30pm–2am. Slot machines are open 12.30–2pm.

Calendar of Special Events

Until the advent of tourism, there were no special events in Seychelles for which visitors would time their holidays; the only exception being the usual Catholic festivals, some of which involve modest parades. Public holidays are mainly religious or political, and celebrations are low-key. The town is illuminated for Christmas and New Year and for most of June, when there are four public holidays, including Independence Day and National Day. A few events have started in recent years which do attract tourists in addition to the locals, and some could merit a special consideration for the tourist. As some dates vary from year to year, check with the respective organisations or the Seychelles Tourism Division in Victoria, Mahé.

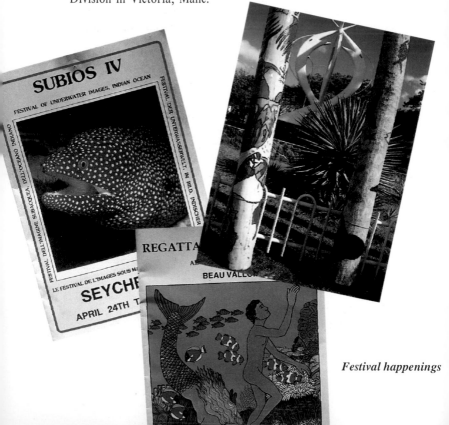

Festival happenings

APRIL – MAY

Fishing Competitions: The National Fishing Competition, organised by the Rotary Club of Victoria, PO Box 395, Victoria (tel: 224206), is held in April each year. Other competitions are held from time to time by the Marine Charter Association, PO Box 469, Victoria (tel: 322126). It is advisable to charter a boat well in advance if you wish to participate. Fishing is a subject dear to the Seychellois soul, and all boats are soon filled during this period.

AUGUST – SEPTEMBER

Beau Vallon Regatta: It is doubtful that you would fly several thousand miles to see it, but there is a 2-day regatta held annually at Beau Vallon on August or September. Depending on your tastes, you might see this as a definite plus, or a big minus if you are staying at one of the Beau Vallon hotels, so it is worth bearing in mind when you choose your holiday dates. The regatta is organised by the Seychelles Round Table and may include a yacht race, swimming competition and other fun competitions such as an underwater treasure hunt, beach tug-of-war and eating and drinking contests.

Evening entertainment may include live music, a fashion show and perhaps a magic show. There are stalls selling food and drink, including beer, and other stalls with simple games typical of any fair. For more details, contact the Seychelles Round Table in Mahé.

Tourism Week: This event takes place in the last week in September. There are bands, *moutya* evenings, cultural evenings, and various events of local colour at the hotels.

OCTOBER

Kreol Festival: The biggest cultural event of the year is the Kreol Festival, held in the last week of October. Created by the Bannzil Kreol Association in 1985, this is an international gathering of Creole artists from countries with a similar cultural background to Seychelles, including Mauritius and the Caribbean. The capital city of Victoria is decorated with colourful posters and other more offbeat items. There are dances, concerts, plays and processions to entertain the crowds.

A great deal of it has little to do with Seychelles' cultural heritage in particular, but the festival is helping to mould a sense of national identity in a young country; together with an awareness of how Seychelles fits in with the rest of the world.

More details can be obtained from the Kreol Festival Committee, Ministry of Education, Mont Fleuri, Mahé (tel: 224777).

NOVEMBER

Subios: The big event of the year for divers is SUBIOS, the Indian Ocean Festival of Underwater Images, held in November each year over a period of three weeks. Entertainment and activities, centred around the main hotels of Mahé and Praslin, include underwater films and talks by the world's diving experts. There is an underwater photography contest with prizes, usually donated by local companies. Dive centres run inshore and long range dives for the participants. Further details can be obtained from travel agents, the Ministry of Tourism, Independence House, Victoria (tel: 224030), or the Seychelles Underwater Centre, Beau Vallon (tel: 345445).

Practical Information

GETTING THERE

By Air

Unless you arrive by ship, you will fly to Seychelles and land at Seychelles International Airport, built on reclaimed land at Pointe Larue on the east coast of Mahé.

Air Seychelles flies non-stop from London twice weekly. The airline also operates four non-stop flights from Paris, two from Johannesburg, one from Rome, one from Zurich and Frankfurt, and one from Singapore. Air Seychelles head office in Mahé can be contacted at tel: 381300. For more details check www.airseychelles.com.

Upmarket cruising on the Renaissance

Air Seychelles and Air Mauritius operate a joint service between their two countries three times a week

Kenya Airways has two flights a week from Nairobi, offering connections from Nairobi to Europe. Air Australe operates one flight a week to Reunion and Aeroflot one flight a week from Moscow via Dubai.

In addition, charter flights to Europe may operate during peak seasons, particularly for Christmas and New Year.

The cheapest direct flights are usually with Air Seychelles. Cheap deals are also available from Kenya Airways, which give the opportunity of combining a Seychelles beach holiday with an East African wildlife safari. If time is no object, rock bottom fares are usually offered by Aeroflot, as the trip involves an overnight stay in Moscow.

By Sea

Several cruiseship companies offer cruises around the islands, mainly from November to March. The companies concerned, and their itineraries, vary from one year to the next. If it is a cruise you are after, then contact your local travel agent to enquire about the latest details. Companies with regular cruises include **Starline Cruises Ltd**, Mombasa (Kenya, tel: 254-11-485220), offering trips connecting Seychelles to other countries in the western Indian Ocean.

Many of the major cruiseship companies include a call at Seychelles in their itineraries. Some of these are round-the-world cruises, while others have a more regional flavour. Apart from Starline Cruises, which is based in the region, all calls are done during the northern winter, mainly November to March.

TRAVEL ESSENTIALS

When to Visit

Any time of year, although the rainiest period of mid-December to end of January is best avoided. Some hotels also charge a supplement during this peak period and again during Easter and August, coinciding with holidays in Europe.

The nicest times are during the calmer months between the two monsoons; April–May or October–November. Calm seas make for pleasant crossings and excellent visibility for snorkelers and divers. April–May is a good time for bird-watchers to catch the beginning of the breeding season for most seabirds. October is the best month for seeing migrant birds.

July–September is also very pleasant, though strong winds make some beaches difficult or dangerous for swimming and sea passages bumpy.

Visas and Passports

You will need a valid international passport with at least six months left on it. Visas are not required by any nationality. An airport tax is included in the cost of your ticket.

Vaccinations

No vaccinations are essential, although some doctors recommend polio and typhoid shots. There is no malaria, yellow fever or other fearsome tropical diseases in Seychelles.

Customs

Visitors are permitted two litres of alcohol, 250g of tobacco or 400 cigarettes and 200ml of perfume. Firearms – including spear guns – fruit and animal products are banned.

Weather

There is no winter, spring or autumn in Seychelles. It is summer all year round, with temperatures varying little from one month to the next in the range 24–30°C (75–86°F). What does vary considerably is the humidity and rainfall. The islands are so green and attractive because rainfall is high, particularly during the northwest monsoon, November–April, reaching a peak from mid-December to the end of January.

Heavy showers are possible at any time of year. Humidity is highest in April, in the lull before the start of the southeast monsoon from May–October. Humidity is lowest during the southeast monsoon. The mountains are generally cooler with far higher rainfall. Mahé and Silhouette have the highest rainfall levels because they are more mountainous than the others.

Clothing

Sunglasses, shorts, T-shirts and flip flops are standard. A sun hat is useful. Do not wander around town or board buses and taxis in swimwear or without a top. The Seychellois take offence. Warm clothing is not needed except if you are venturing out to sea at night.

Some hotels require men to wear long trousers in public areas after 7.30pm. A jacket and tie are not required, even for

Life's a beach

businessmen, unless you are joining a cruise ship. Ladies do not need sophisticated evening gowns; simple, cool cotton dresses will do.

Electricity

Seychelles' electrical current is 240 volts AC. Sockets are three point (square pin), the same as in UK. A torch can be useful as power cuts are fairly frequent.

Time Differences

Seychelles time is 4 hours ahead of Greenwich Mean Time (GMT).

Perpetual summer and sunny skies

Geography

Seychelles consists of 155 islands with a total land mass of 455sq km (176sq miles). They spread over an Exclusive Economic Zone of 1,340,000sq km (517,400 sq miles).

Granite outcrops at Curieuse

The main islands, where 99 percent of Seychellois live, are the world's only granitic outcrops in mid-ocean, all other ocean islands being either volcanic or coralline in origin. Their origin can be traced back to the super-continent of Pangaea which encompassed all the world's continents 200 million years ago. Pangaea broke up, forming Laurasia to the north – modern North America, Europe and Asia, and Gondwanaland – the southern continents – to the south. India, wedged between Madagascar and Africa on one side and Antarctica to the other, broke off and drifted across what was the Sea of Tethys, now the Indian Ocean. Seychelles broke away from the western edge of India close to the Deccan Plateau, and was thus isolated.

In addition, there are many coral islands. Closest to the granitic group are Bird and Denis, both of which can be reached by air from Mahé. They are sand cays, with no barrier reef.

South of Mahé lie Platte and Coetivy, two isolated coral islands. Approximately 200km (125 miles) west of Mahé is the Amirantes chain – an arc of coral platform islands and atolls covering an area of ocean approximately 180km (113 miles) by 35km (22 miles). Beyond the Amirantes is the Farquhar Group. Farquhar is one of the largest atolls in Seychelles and lies much closer to Madagascar than to Mahé.

Further west again, to the extreme southwestern corner of Seychelles' Exclusive Economic Zone, is the Aldabra group of islands. These are raised limestone platform islands and atolls, up to 8m (26ft) above sea level. This rare type of island was formed when sea levels fell a few thousand years ago due to a change in ocean currents within the Indian Ocean.

Two islands, Silhouette and North, are of volcanic origin.

Economy

Today, the principal source of foreign exchange receipts is tourism. Fishing, especially tuna fishing, is vital to the economy. Much tuna is canned locally for export.

Religion

The vast majority of Seychellois are at least token Roman Catholics, the women taking their faith most seriously. The second largest Christian denomination are the Anglicans. There is also a community of Seventh Day Adventists. Hindu and Muslim faiths are also represented.

Celebrating First Communion

Whom Do You Trust?

On the whole, you can trust nearly everybody. Women travelling alone should use common sense and not allow themselves to be isolated in remote corners with would-be Lotharios. Keep your valuables sensibly protected. Mugging has not yet, thank goodness, become a major feature of Seychelles life but is not unknown.

Victoria taxi rank

You should always take times arranged with Seychellois with a pinch of salt. Tour agents will be fairly reliable, but any friends/acquaintances you make will probably have a fairly loose idea of the meaning of punctuality.

Population

Seychelles has a population of about 80,000. The majority are of African or Malagasy origin, the descendants of slaves or freed slaves.

This population has, over the years, mixed extensively with those of European – mostly French – descent. There have always been Indian elements amongst the Seychellois, and there is also a significant Chinese community. Few Britons ever settled here.

MONEY MATTERS

Currency

The Seychelles rupee is divided into notes of SR100, SR50, SR25 and SR10. Coins come in denominations of SR5, SR1, 25 cents, 10 cents and 5 cents.

Prices in shops will often be in amounts which do not end in units of 5 or 10 cents, and unless you are paying by credit card, will be rounded up or down when you are given change – usually up!

Credit Cards

Major credit cards are accepted at most larger hotels and restaurants. Visa and MasterCard are most commonly accepted.

Tipping

Tipping is not essential in Seychelles. Many hotels and restaurants include a service charge in the bill and this is accepted as sufficient.

Money Changers

Travellers' cheques, Eurocheques and most Western currencies are accepted in Seychelles. You will get a much better rate of exchange from banks than hotels or other establishments.

Foreign exchange transactions may only be made with authorised dealers, including most companies active in the tourism sector, but not taxi drivers. You may be approached and offered a higher rate on the black market, but if caught, penalties are high.

Saymore Bureau de Change, situated immediately on the right as you come through customs at the airport, offer superior exchange rates to the banks.

It is not necessary to have any Seychelles rupees before arrival as airport banks open for all international flights. You will get a higher rate for travellers' cheques than for currency.

According to the law, many transactions for hotels, boats and watersports centres must be paid in foreign exchange.

At press time, the exchange rate was fixed at SR5.50 to US$1.

GETTING AROUND

Taxis

Taxis are plentiful on Mahé, and less common on Praslin and La Digue. Since there are no roads on any other islands, there are, not surprisingly, no taxis either. On Mahé and Praslin, taxis are metered. The driver will normally have to be asked to switch the meter on because the system is not popular. If the meter is not used, make sure a fee is agreed with the taxi driver in advance to avoid any dispute. Drivers are a bit selective about the journeys they are prepared to make; some are unwilling to tackle particularly bad roads or trips out to remote areas. If you negotiate a daily or hourly rate, many of them can be amusing and informative guides to the islands.

Taxis are available at Mahé and Praslin airports, Victoria taxi rank, Albert Street – next door to Camion Hall, and by the Clock Tower in Independence Avenue, Victoria. They are also usually available from larger hotels. Don't expect to hail a taxi at any time of day or night, especially on Praslin or La Digue.

Bus

Buses are cheap and can be a good way to get around if you have time and can avoid the peak periods, but prepare for long waits and a fight for seats on some routes. Timings and routes are geared to suit the local population, not the tourist. Most routes run from about 5.30am to about 7pm, with a reduced service on Sundays and public holidays.

Many buses are past their prime and battle along with a tremendous clash and clatter. Some of the driving is a bit hair-raising too, especially if the bus is almost empty or it is the last run of the day. You can get thrown about a bit on the bends. The services are often unreliable because of breakdowns and limited number of vehicles available.

Car

Many car hire companies are represented at Seychelles International Airport and larger hotels. Rates are fairly standard and are for unlimited mileage. It is wise to book in advance. Cars are not always in best condition. Check brakes and indicators before you set off. Mini Mokes are fun but the seats get wet if it rains and it is harder to secure your valuables.

Valid driving licences issued by any international body are accepted. You do not need an international driving permit in order to hire a vehiche. Driving is on the left unlike in the US and Europe. Road signs are similar, or the same as those in Europe. Beware: if you see what seems to be a tree growing in the middle of the road, it means a huge pot hole has opened up and someone has considerably marked it with a branch. Speed limits are 40kph (25mph) in towns and villages, and 65kph (40mph) outside. The only ex-

ception is along Mahé's east coast road, where the limit is 80kph (50mph).

Roads are narrow, usually with deep drainage ditches at the side. Mountain roads are steep with many very sharp bends. On Mahé, the standard of road maintenance is high. Some roads on Praslin are not so good.

Driving standards and road discipline are sloppy. Pedestrians seem oblivious to cars, especially during the weekends or public holidays when the beer has flowed a little too freely.

Victoria Service Station is open daily 5.30am–11pm; **Beau Vallon Service Station** daily 6am–9pm; and **Grand Anse, Praslin Service Station** Monday–Saturday 7.30am–6pm, and Sunday and public holidays 7.30am–noon. Parking is free, except in Victoria, where street parking costs SR2, limited to 30 minutes and car parks have a variable rate according to time. Parking on the Stadium Car Park is free. Tickets are available from many retail outlets. Prices apply Monday to Saturday 8am–6pm.

Ferry

A 25-metre fast, air-conditioned catamaran ferry, **Cat Cocos**, operates between Mahé and Praslin. Journey time is less than 1 hour. There is a upper deck Club Lounge with 34 seats and a Main Cabin with 125. Both cabins have video and audio entertainment, and a bar serves snacks and drinks. It operates daily with up to three trips in each direction per day. For times of departures call **Inter Island Boats** (Mahé tel: 324843, Praslin tel: 233438).

Schooner ferries also run between the main islands of Mahé, Praslin and La Digue. The schooner *La Belle Praslinoise* takes 3 hours to cross from Praslin to

Mahé while *Cousin* takes 2½ hours. *La Belle Edma* takes 3¼ hours between La Digue and Mahé. These slower ferries generally depart Praslin or La Digue between 5am and 6am, returning from Mahé around noon the same day. An inter-island ferry schedule can be collected from the **Tourism Division**, Ground Floor, Independence House, Independence Avenue, Victoria. Alternatively, call the ferry owner.

La Belle Praslinoise (Mr L Grandcourt), tel: 233512.
Cousin (Mr J Adrienne), tel: 233343.
La Belle Edma (Mr E Mussad), tel: 234013.

The regular ferry from Praslin to La Digue departs at 7am, 9am, 10am, 11am, 2.30pm, 4pm and 5.15pm. The return trip to Praslin departs at 7.30am, 9.30am, 10.30am, noon, 3.30pm, 4.30pm and 5.45pm. For bookings, contact **Inter-Island Ferry Service** (tel: 233229).

The ferry terminal on Mahé is the Inter-Island Quay, on Praslin the Baie Ste Anne Jetty, and on La Digue the La Passe Jetty. Do not rely on taxis being available at the other end. Telephone in advance and give the taxi driver your arrival time (see *Getting Around*).

Helicopter

There are scheduled helicopter flights to La Digue, departing from the Domestic Terminal, Monday, Wednesday, Thursday, Friday and Saturday. Departure times are subject to revision, and should be checked. A maximum of four passengers can be carried. It is often possible to turn up without booking, should you decide it's a great day to visit La Digue, but it is better to book in advance and avoid disappointment.

Transfers to Silhouette can also be arranged on Sunday mornings. These are principally for guests of Silhouette Island Lodge and bookings should be made through the **Silhouette Island Lodge** (tel: 224003).

Transfers between certain islands and hotels may also be arranged. For these and La Digue transfers, contact **Helicopter Seychelles** (tel: 373900).

Domestic Flights

Air Seychelles operate many flights in small planes (maximum 20 passengers) daily between Mahé and Praslin, 6.45am–9.30pm (Mahé to Praslin) and 7.15am–

10pm (Praslin to Mahé). Flights operate between Mahé and hotels on Alphonse, Bird, Denis, Desroches and Frégate and are booked as part of a package with the hotels concerned.

Mahé flights depart from the Domestic Terminal, at the north end of Seychelles International Airport. Flight time is 15 minutes to Praslin, 15 minutes to Frégate, 30 minutes to Bird or Denis, 45 minutes to Desroches and one hour to Alphonse.

Special charters and photographic flights are also available. For further information contact **Air Seychelles** (tel: 381300).

By Yacht or Motorboat

Day trips can be arranged to most islands; those further afield require boats with live aboard facilities. Details can be obtained from **Marine Charter Association** (tel: 322126). See *Activities* for other contacts.

Bicycle

Unless you are a budding Olympic champion, Mahé by bike is not recommended. The roads are very steep, busy and narrow. Praslin is less busy and less mountainous. Cycles are available at Baie Ste Anne, Anse Volbert and Grand Anse. Bicycles are the way to see La Digue, where they can be hired almost everywhere, but the biggest selection is at La Passe.

Inter-island planes

Business Hours

Office hours are Monday–Friday 8am–4pm. Shop hours are 8.30am/9am–5/5.30pm Monday–Friday and 8.30am/9am–noon Saturday. Many shops close for lunch 12.30–1.30pm. Some shops, mainly Indian merchants outside town, are open on Saturday afternoon, Sunday and public holidays.

Public Holidays

1–2 January: New Year
March/April: Good Friday
1 May: Labour Day
5 June: Liberation Day
18 June: National Day
Mid-June: Corpus Christi
29 June: Independence Day
15 August: Assumption
1 November: All Saints Day
8 December: Immaculate Conception
25 December: Christmas

ACCOMMODATION

Hotels

There is no official star rating system in Seychelles. Room standards are generally high but standards of service are often poor. Prices are high and you are usually better off with a package deal than paying the official rack rates. Peak season supplements may apply at Easter, Christmas/New Year and in August. It is illegal to camp or sleep rough anywhere in Seychelles.

Price categories for a double room, per night, inclusive of breakfast are:

$ = SR500 and below
$$ = SR500–1,000
$$$ = SR1,000–2,000
$$$$ = SR2,000 and above

There is no such thing as budget accommodation in Seychelles, but the best deals are often obtainable by purchasing a package deal. There is no service charge or tax.

Mahé

ALLAMANDA HOTEL
Anse Forbans, Mahé
Tel: 366266

e-mail: amanda@seychelles.net
www.the-seychelles.com/allamanda
A beautiful small colonial-style hotel of just ten rooms, all air-conditioned, situated in the quiet southern end of the island. Anse Forbans beach is ideal for swimming and snorkelling. *$$*

Banyan Tree Resort

BANYAN TREE RESORT
Anse Intendance, Mahé
Tel: 383500
e-mail: seychelles@banyantree.com
www.banyantree.com
The most modern hotel on Mahé (opened 2001) and the highest of standards. There are 37 villas and one Presidential villa, all set in lush tropical surroundings on a hillside overlooking a beautiful beach in a quiet corner of the main island. *$$$$*

CHATEAU D'EAU
PO Box 107, Barbarons, Mahé
Tel: 378177, Fax: 378388
Opposite side of Mahé to the airport and Victoria, so it is nice and peaceful. Very pleasant location. Expensive for a guest house, but standards are high. *$$$*

LA RESIDENCE
Anse a la Mouche
Tel: 371370, Fax: 371370
www.the-seychelles.com/residence
Made up of three villas and three apartments, each with two bedrooms and self-catering facilities. The rooms are not air-conditioned, but have ceiling fans and overlook a magnificent bay. *$$*

LE MERIDIEN FISHERMAN'S COVE HOTEL
PO Box 35, Bel Ombre, Mahé
Tel: 247252

e-mail: fishres@seychelles.net
www.lemeridien-fishcove.com
Facing Beau Vallon beach, this is a small, upmarket hotel with a club-like atmosphere. There are 48 rooms (all with direct access to the beach), with air-conditioning, telephone, radio, TV and en suite facilities. There are three tennis courts – two with night lighting. Guests may have a free introductory diving lesson with Seychelles Underwater Centre. $$$$

NORTH POINT GUESTHOUSE
Fonds des Lianes, Machabée
Tel: 241339, Fax: 241850
Situated on the northern tip of Mahé, with dramatic views across to Silhouette and North islands. A friendly, cosy guest house with self-catering apartments and also a restaurant offering breakfast and dinners if required. There is a delightful small beach accessible only from the guest house. There are just eight apartments, including one family apartment for four people. $

ROSE GARDEN HOTEL
Sans Souci, Mahé
Tel: 225308, Fax: 226245
e-mail: rosgdn@seychelles.net
Tucked well away from the beach, in the cool exhilarating atmosphere of the mountains. Spectacular views. $

Praslin

CHATEAU DE FEUILLES
Pointe Cabris, Baie Ste Anne
Tel: 233916
e-mail: info@chateau.com.sc
www.chateau.com.sc
A small and exclusive hotel set in a beautiful garden on a quiet headland with superb panoramic views. Its nine rooms are lavishly furnished with every conceivable mod-con. A free car is provided to guests and at weekends there is the chance to visit, by helicopter, the private island of Grande Souer for swimming and a barbeque lunch. $$$$

COCO DE MER HOTEL
Anse Bois de Rose, Praslin
Tel: 233900
www.cocodemer.com

This resort is located between Grand Anse and Baie Ste Anne on its own beautiful beach. There are 30 spacious rooms, all with sea views, bathroom, sitting area and balcony or terrace. Each has telephone, TV and air-conditioning. Facilities include windsurfing, canoes, a tennis court, bicycles and various games. $$$

INDIAN OCEAN LODGE
Grand Anse, Praslin
Tel: 233324, 233457
e-mail: hmcom@seychelles.net
Situated right on the beach, just 5 minutes from the airport. There are 16 sea-view rooms and eight suites, all air-conditioned with telephone and en suite bathroom. Watersports facilities – windsurfing, paddle skis and snorkelling equipment – are free to all in-house residents. $$$

L'ARCHIPEL
Anse Gouvernement, Praslin
Tel: 232242
www.larchipel.com
A beautiful small hotel with 21 rooms and three suites, set on the hillside, with views of Curieuse and Anse Gouvernement. Sheltered waters mean swimming is possible year round. Rooms are spacious and the cuisine is excellent. $$$$

LEMURIA RESORT
Anse Kerlan, Praslin
Tel: 281281
e-mail: lemuria@seychelles.net
www.constancehotels.com
This luxury resort in an idyllic location is possibly the best hotel in Seychelles. Facilities include a golf course, fully equipped business centre, jacuzzi, sauna, children's club and all the usual hotel and watersports options you would expect from a five-star hotel. There are three beaches, and all 88 suites, eight villas and a presidential villa face the ocean. $$$$

Coral Strand Hotel

VILLA FLAMBOYANT
Anse St Sauveur, Praslin
Tel/Fax: 233036
Beautiful location, right on a quiet beach. Guests are made very much part of the family. Friendly atmosphere and good home cooking. Free art tuition for residents. *$$*

VILLAS DE MER
Grand Anse, Praslin
Tel: 233972, Fax: 233015
Good, clean, simple facilities provided in pleasant chalets by the sea. The cost of breakfast is included and dinner can be provided by arrangement if you like. Guests are given a tour of the local shops on arrival. Snorkelling equipment available. Friendly atmosphere. *$*

Villas De Mer's beachside chalets

La Digue

CHATEAU ST CLOUD
Anse Reunion, La Digue
Tel: 234346
e-mail: stcloud@seychelles.net
The chateau is not a typical, modern hotel but instead retains the charm of its colonial past when it formed part of a vanilla plantation. For those who wish to stay on La Digue to better enjoy its quaint lifestyle, this is certainly a little different to a modern hotel. *$$*

HOTEL L'OCEAN
Anse Patates, La Digue
Tel: 234180
e-mail: hocean@seychelles.net
www.hotelocean.info
Situated in a stunning location on the northern tip of La Digue with views over Anse Sévère and Anse Patates. There are eight rooms, each with private veranda and beautiful ocean views.

LA DIGUE ISLAND LODGE
Anse Reunion, La Digue
Tel: 234232
www.ladigue.sc
Situated near the picturesque beach of Anse Reunion within a short distance of the jetty. There are 60 rooms, with an amazing variety of accommodation: A-frame chalets or bungalows for families, villas with private verandahs and the marvellously eccentric eight-room colonial house known as the Yellow House, with two floors and a spiral staircase. *$$$$*

Other Islands

Each of these islands has just one hotel and (apart from Silhouette) no other inhabitants. These islands offer a marked contrast with the larger, more developed and inhabited islands of Seychelles.

ALPHONSE ISLAND RESORT
Tel: 323220 (Victoria Head Office),
Tel: 229030 (Alphonse)
e-mail: alphonse@seychelles.net
Very high standards in the ultimate remote setting. There are 25 thatched chalets and 5 executive suites, all air-conditioned and equipped with everything from satellite TV to jacuzzi. Activities include superb fly-fishing and diving. Excellent restaurant as well. *$$$$*

ANONYME ISLAND RESORT
Tel: 380100
e-mail: anonyme@seychelles.net
Six spacious suites and one Presidential villa, offering a flavour of a remote island, yet just a few minutes from Mahé. Located near to the airport, this is an excellent place to spend the final day of your vacation. Enjoy the rare experience of taking a boat ride to the airport in Mahé to catch your flight. *$$$$*

Alphonse Island Resort

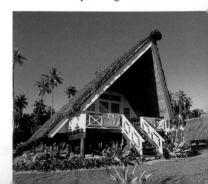

BIRD ISLAND LODGE
Tel: 224925 (Victoria Head Office),
Tel: 323322 (Bird Island)
e-mail: birdland@seychelles.net
www.BirdIslandSeychelles.com
Comfortable individual chalets with ceiling fans on an island that lives up to its name. The restaurant is excellent. *$$$*

Bird Island Lodge

COUSINE ISLAND
Tel: 321107
e-mail: cousine@seychelles.net
www.indianoceanislands.net
There are just four luxurious villas on this exceptional private nature reserve, which is otherwise closed to the public. A warden employed by the hotel takes guided tours on request. There is a swimming pool and the beach is also excellent for swimming. *$$$$*

DENIS ISLAND
Tel: 321143
e-mail: denis@seychelles.net
Has 20 spacious, air-conditioned chalets. Excellent watersports and diving on the edge of the Seychelles Bank. It is possible to swim within a short stroll of each chalet. *$$$$*

DESROCHES ISLAND RESORT
Tel: 229009 (Mahé Head Office),
Tel: 229003 (Desroches Island)
e-mail: desroches@seychelles.net
Has 20 spacious air-conditioned chalets. Good diving, especially November–April and non-motorised waterports within the safety of the lagoon. *$$$$*

FÉLICITE PRIVATE ISLAND
Contact details and website are the same as La Digue Lodge (*see page 88*), which provides diving and watersports facilities

if required. This is the ultimate in privacy with just two bungalows and accommodation for 2–10 people. When one group of any size makes a booking, no other bookings are accepted for those same dates. *$$$$*

FREGATE ISLAND PRIVATE
Tel: 324545 (Mahé Head Office),
Tel: 323370 (Frégate Island)
e-mail: fregate@seychelles.net
www.fregate.com
Sixteen luxury villas (and a maximum of 40 guests) each with a view of the ocean on beautiful granite island. Golf carts are available to explore well-marked tracks to the plantation, the woodland and the island's seven beaches. This is the ultimate – if you can afford it. *$$$$*

NORTH ISLAND LODGE
Tel: 293100, Fax: 293150
e-mail: info@north-island.com
www.north-island.com
This is the place for nature lovers who enjoy luxury: a combination of a five-star resort and a conservation project, where endangered Seychelles flora and fauna is being reintroduced. There are just 11 villas, reached by a 2-hour boat journey or 20 minutes by helicopter. *$$$$*

SILHOUETTE ISLAND LODGE
Tel: 344154 (Mahé Head Office),
Tel: 224003 (Silhouette Island)
e-mail: sillodge@seychelles.net
www.silhouette-seychelles.com
Silhouette is actually the third largest island and only Mahé rises higher. However, it has a tiny population and remains relatively pristine. An overnight stay is the best way to explore this beautiful island and its mountains and beaches. *$$$$*

ST ANNE RESORT
Tel: 292000, Fax: 292002
e-mail: res.sa@bchot.com
www.sainteanne-resort.com
This modern five-star resort is connected to Mahé by a regular ferry. There are 82 one-bedroom villas, four two-bedroom and one three-bedroom. Facilities include tennis, mountain bikes, deep-sea fishing and a variety of watersports. *$$$$*

HEALTH & EMERGENCIES

Hygiene/General Health

Water in tourist establishments is generally safe to drink and the standard of hygiene is good.

You will almost certainly be bitten by mosquitoes, though these are only really active around dusk. Apply insect repellent or light a mosquito coil, which is usually available in the hotel room.

Black wasps are harmless but yellow wasps can leave the victim with an extremely painful sting. Avoid going near their nests, which are cone-shaped and hang from tree branches. Also, give large centipedes a wide berth.

High factor sun creams are essential. Do not underestimate the power of the overhead sun. Drink plenty of liquids and not all beer or cola, which can dehydrate you. You should make a point of drinking at least a glass or two of water if you've been out on the beach all day.

The dangers of the deep for the tourist are minimal. Black sea urchins are perhaps the greatest menace. Their spines can be dissolved out of your skin by applying a little pawpaw. Cone shells have extremely painful and toxic stings. If you pick any up, even those which seem to be dead, do so by the thick end, keeping the pointed end – where the harpoon is – well away from your body. Always wear plastic shoes or other suitable footwear if you are walking over coral rock. Coral cuts can be very slow to heal. Some live corals and fish sting. If in doubt, it is far better not to touch, just look.

Pharmacies

There are two fairly reliable pharmacies in Victoria, Mahé:
Behram's Pharmacy, Victoria Arcade, Victoria, tel: 225559 and **Le Chantier**, Victoria, tel: 224093.
Lai Lam (Pty) Ltd, Market Street, Victoria, tel: 322336.

Bring prescription medicines with you, but if you do run out, try the Dispensary at the **Outpatients Department**, **Victoria Hospital** or **Le Chantier Medical Services**, Le Chantier, Victoria (Mon-

day–Friday 8am–7pm closed 1–2pm, Saturday 8am–1pm, tel: 324008, 322831). There are no pharmacies on Praslin. Go to the nearest hospital dispensary.

Medical/Dental Services

Health services are fairly good in Seychelles. Larger hotels have nurses who can arrange a visit to the tourist doctor if necessary. Normal consultation hours are 8am–4pm and there is a small fee payable. There are also a limited number of private clinics. One of these, **Le Chantier Medical Services**, (*see above*) also offers a dental clinic.

Victoria Hospital is south of the town, next to the Botanical Gardens. There are also hospitals at Anse Royale, Mahé, on Praslin and La Digue, together with local clinics in many villages.
Useful numbers are:
Victoria Hospital, tel: 388000.
Anse Royale Hospital, tel: 371222.
Praslin Hospital, tel: 232333.
Logan Hospital, La Digue, tel: 234255.

Crime

Violent crime involving tourists is rare but casual theft is on the increase. Do not leave valuables unguarded, especially at the beach when swimming. Lock your hotel room and car. Take the same common sense precautions you would take almost everywhere these days. The same applies to women travelling alone. Do not be fooled into thinking that because Seychelles looks like paradise.

Police

Central Police Station – the headquarters – is in Revolution Avenue, Victoria. Dial 999 in an emergency; same for Fire Brigade and Ambulance. Useful numbers:
Central Police Station, Mahé, tel: 288000.
Beau Vallon Police Station, Mahé, tel: 247242.
Grand Anse Police Station, Praslin tel: 233251.

Baie Ste Anne Police Station, Praslin, tel: 232332.
La Digue Police Station, tel: 234251.

Post

The main post office in Victoria is open Monday–Friday 8am–4pm and Saturday 8am–noon. Most hotels sell stamps and will post mail for you. There are post boxes by police stations in the villages.

Telephone

International direct dialling is available to most countries. Public telephones are plentiful and **Cable & Wireless** (tel: 284064) in Victoria is open Monday to Saturday, 7am–9pm, for telephone, fax and telex services. This is worth bearing in mind as hotels generally impose a 100 percent surcharge on call costs, which are already much higher in Seychelles than elsewhere. Most public phones take only phonecards, on sale at Cable & Wireless and many shops. Some of the more remote islands have no phone service, although an increasing number are having satellite phone links installed.

You can use your mobile phone in Seychelles if you have a roaming facility (check with your service provider). Local mobile phone numbers begin with a '5' or '7'. Useful numbers are:
Seychelles country code: 248.
IDD (from Seychelles): 00
International Flight Enquiries, tel: 384400.

Domestic Flight Enquiries, tel: 381340.
Praslin Airport, tel: 284666.
Met Office (weather), tel: 373377.
Operator, dial: 100.
International Operator, dial: 151.
Directory Enquiries, dial: 181.

Media

There is one daily (except Sunday and public holidays) newspaper, the government-managed *Seychelles Nation*. The independent newspaper *Regar* is published weekly on Thursdays. Articles in *Seychelles Nation* are in English, French and Creole. Articles in *Regar* are mainly in English. There are two local terrestrial TV stations, Seychelles Broadcasting Corporation and a French language station. Many hotels have satellite TV.

Weddings

If you can't face your in-laws to be and all those awful relatives, or you just want to get married in one of the world's most romantic destinations, Seychelles could be the perfect choice for your wedding. Assuming the whole thing is not spontaneous, book through a tour operator, who will arrange everything from the hotel to the cake, wedding photography, live music and so on.

If it is all a bit spur of the moment, you can still make arrangements on site. We once ended up at the wedding of a rock musician who arranged a last minute surprise wedding for his girlfriend who

thought she was just visiting friends for dinner. In approximately 5 minutes from proposal to pronouncement they were man and wife. On Mahé, contact the **Registrar** (tel: 225333) at the Civil Status Division, Independence House, Victoria, for do-it-yourself weddings. You will need your birth certificates, passports, and if applicable, divorce papers. You need to be in Seychelles a minimum of 11 days to be eligible. If you can't be bothered to make your own arrangements, contact a reputable local travel agent.

On the outer islands, we recommend **Alphonse Island Resort**. This is the most beautiful, romantic island, ideal for a wedding away from it all. Contact the Head Office on Mahé (*see Accommodation, Other Islands*), which can arrange all the formalities, including a photographer if required.

Travel agents can also arrange weddings at other locations including Mahé and the smaller islands.

Children

Seychelles is a fun place for children, if only because of the lovely beaches and opportunities to play in the sea. The Seychellois love children. It is one of the best ways of making friends locally. There is nothing to worry about from a health point of view, except the fierce strength of the sun. Try and get the children to keep a hat on. It is quite safe to bring a babe in arms here and a mobile child who can enjoy the sea and sand, but for the ages in between, it could be a wasted experience. Older children will have loads of fun with the watersports.

Maps

Detailed island maps are on sale at the **Survey Division**, Ground Floor, Independence House, Victoria.

Bookshops

There are few bookshops in Seychelles, although most gift shops will sell a range of books about Seychelles. The best bookshop is **Antigone**, located at Passage des Palmes, Victoria House, Victoria. In addition to books about Seychelles, you will also find novels in English and French. The bookshop also has kiosks at the International Airport and Inter-Island Terminal.

Other bookshops include **Memorabilia**, Revolution Avenue, Victoria. European newspapers and magazines, a little out of date, can be bought at **Antigone**.

Family fun under the sun

Photography

Film can be purchased at reasonable prices in Seychelles, though hotel shops tend to be more expensive. Kodak and Fuji films are available here through **Photo Eden** and **Kim Koon** respectively, in Independence Avenue, Victoria, Mahé. Same-day processing is available for both prints and slides, but it is fairly expensive and often of poor quality.

LANGUAGE

Seychelles is trilingual: English, French and Creole are spoken. On Mahé you will have little trouble in getting by in English or French, but elsewhere a few words of Creole can help. Creole is mainly French in origin and most of the nouns will be familiar if you speak French. But the grammar is much simpler, with only one form for each verb, no sexes and no need to worry about your accent. It is written phonetically and every letter is pronounced.

English	Creole
Yes	Wi
No	Non
Hello	Bonzour
How are you?	Sava / Ki i dir?
I am well	Mon byen
Thank you	Mersi
Good afternoon	Bon apremidi
Goodbye	Orevwar
What is this?	Kisisa?
I don't understand	Mon pa konpran
Could you repeat that please?	Repete sivouple
Good	Bon
Bad	Pa bon
I don't know	Mon pa konnen
I'm hungry	Mon lafen
I'm thirsty	Mon swaf
Where is the hotel?	Kote lotel sivouple?
Where are you from?	Kote ou sorti?
I like...	Mon kontan avek...
How much?	Kombyen i vann?
That's expensive	I ser
A little bit	En ti pe
Where is the toilet?	Kote kabinen sivouple?
When?	Kan?
How?	Ki mannyer?
Why?	Akoz?
Which?	Lekel?
Shop	Laboutik
You	Ou
We	Nou
What?	Ki? / Kwa?
Who?	Ki? / Lekel?

Grafitti art on corrugated fence

USEFUL ADDRESSES

Tourist Office

SEYCHELLES TOURISM DIVISION
Ministry of Tourism and Civil Aviation,
Victoria, Mahé, Seychelles
Tel: 224030; email: tgtmca@seychelles.net
www.aspureasitgets.com

Travel Agents

7° SOUTH
Kingsgate Travel Centre
Independence Avenue, Victoria
Tel: 322682/322292
e-mail: 7south@seychelles.net
www.7south.net

MASONS TRAVEL
Michel Bldg, Revolution Avenue, Victoria
Tel: 322642/322407
e-mail: masons@seychelles.net
www.masonstravel.com

TRAVEL SERVICES SEYCHELLES
Mahe Trading Bldg, Victoria
Tel: 322414
e-mail: tss@tss.sc; www.tss.sc

Useful Websites

www.sey.net
www.airseychelles.com
www.seychelles.net
www.aspureasitgets.com

Index

A

accommodation 86–89
activities 61–67
Aldabra 67
Alphonse 59–60
Amirantes Trench 59
Anonyme Island 38
Anse à la Mouche 20, 28, 35, 63
Anse aux Pins 25, 35, 62
Anse aux Poules Bleues 28
Anse Banane 48
Anse Bateau 43
Anse Boudin 44
Anse Cimitiére 37, 43
Anse Citron 43
Anse Consolation 43
Anse du Riz 34
Anse Fourmis 48
Anse Grosse Roche 48
Anse Gaulettes 48
Anse La Blague 44
Anse la Passe 38
Anse Lascars 37
Anse Lazio 42, 44
Anse Madge 43
Anse Major 61, 62
Anse Marie Louise 27, 43
Anse Mondon 37
Anse Patates 48
Anse Possession 44
Anse Royale 26–27, 35
Anse Sévère 48
Anse Soleil 28
Anse St José 53, 54
Anse Takamaka 43
Anse Union 49
Anse Volbert 39
Aride 39, 44, 49–52
    Viewing Point 51
    Visitors' Shelter 50–51
Auberge Club des Seychelles 62, 65

B

Baie Lazare 27
Baie Lazare Church 27
Baie Ste Anne 39, 43
Baie Ternay Marine National Park 33, 34
Barbara Jenson Studio 48
Beau Vallon 20, 21, 28, 29, 33, 35, 38,
    62, 64–66
Bel Air Cemetery 24
Bel Ombre 23, 29, 62
Belle Vue 47
Bijoutier 59–60
Bird 55, 56
    Viewing Platform 55

C

Cape Barbi 48
Cerf 34–35
Chateau St Cloud 47
Congo Range 63
Copolia 29

Cousin 39, 52–53
Craft Village 25
Curieuse 39, 44, 53, 54
   Doctor's House 53

D

Danzil River 62
Dauban Mausoleum 37
Desroches 57–58
   dive centre 57
   Lighthouse 58
   Settlement 57–58
Donald Adelaide 27

E – G

Eating out 72–76
Ecomusee La Plaine St Andre 26
Flycatcher Reserve 47
Fond Ferdinand 43
Galerie des Artes 44
Gérard Devoud's Art Studio 27
Grand Anse 28, 39, 42, 49, 54
Grand Anse River 49
Green Gecko Gallery 48

H – J

Ile aux Vaches 63
Ile Cahée 35
Intendance 20, 27, 35
Island Conservation Society 49
Isle of Farquhar 25
Jardin du Roi 26–27

K – L

Kreol' Or 25
L'Union Estate 48
La Digue 20, 25, 35, 39, 45–49
La Digue Cross 46
La Digue Rock 48–49
La Mare Soupape 49
La Marine 26

La Passe 36, 46, 49
   plantation house 37
Laraie Bay 54
Lensiti Kreol 62
Long 35

M

Mahé 20–39, 64
Maison Coco 25
Maison du Peuple 44
Maison St Joseph 25
Michael Adams Studio 28
Mission Historical Ruins and Viewing
   Point 29
Morne Blanc 29, 35, 63
Morne Seychellois 34, 35, 63
Morne Seychellois National Park 28, 35,
   63
Moyenne 35

N – P

Nature Protection Trust of Seychelles 37
nightlife 76 78
North 36, 38
obelisk 24
Pineapple Studio 28
Pointe Cabriz 43
Pointe Cocos 43
Pointe Source d'Argent 49
Pointe Zeng Zeng 37
Priest's Residence 32
Praslin 20, 25, 35, 39–54
Praslin National Park 39

Q – R

Quatre Bornes 27
Rat Island 38
Roman Catholic Cathedral 32
Round 34–35, 38
Royal Spice Garden 26–27

S

Sans Souci 21, 28–29, 63
Sentier Vacoa Trail 28
Seychelles Tea and Coffee Company 28, 63
Seychelles Underwater Centre 64
shopping 68–71
Signal Hill 23
Silhouette 20, 36, 63
St Anne Marine National Park 20, 24–25, 33–35, 38, 63
St Francois 59–60
St Pierre 53–54

T

Takamaka 20, 27, 35
The Drop 57
Thoughts Stained Glass Studio 24
Tom Sculpture Studio 28
Trois Frères 29
Trois Frères Trail 29
Tuna Quay 35

U – Z

Unity Stadium 35
Vallée de Mai 30, 39, 41–44, 62
    Circular Path 41–42
    Information Centre 41
    National Park 41
Victoria 23–25, 29, 30–33, 38, 62
    Botanical Gardens 30
    Camian Hall 31
    Clock Tower 31–32
    Court House 31
    Hindu Temple 32
    Independence House 33
    Kaz Zanana 23, 29, 32
    Kenwyn House 30
    National Museum of Natural History, The 32–33
    Seychelles National Museum of History, The 32
    Sir Selwyn Selwyn Clarke Market 32
    Stadium Car Park 30
    Tourism Division Shop 33
Villa Flamboyant 43
water wheel 25

ACKNOWLEDGMENTS

Front Cover	**Chad Ehlers/Alamy**
Back Cover (top)	**Seychelles Underwater Centre**
Back Cover (bottom)	**Christine Osborne**
Photography	**Adrian Skerrett** and
Pages 5B, 8/9, 13, 66, 68M, 69 (perfume), 69 (model boats), 70B, 71, 72T, 72B, 73T, 73B, 76, 77T, 81T, 92B	**Christine Osborne**
28B	**Tom Bowers**
10	**Tony Arruza**
34	**Seychelles Underwater Centre**
Handwriting	**V. Barl**
Cover Design	**Klaus Geisler**
Cartography	**Berndtson & Berndtson**